THE
BOOK
BOOK

THE BOOK BOOK:

A Publishing Handbook for Beginners and Others

L. M. Hasselstrom

LJ Press Books:

A Country for Old Men and other stories
fiction about the West by E.R. Zietlow

Homemade Poems: A Handbook to Po[...]
primer for making poems by Daniel [...]k **O.P**

Topographics
poems by Margaret Condon

Next-Year Country: One Woman's View
1920's farm photographs by Alma Phillip

*The Indian Maiden's Captivity/The Heart
of the Country*
two-novel volume by E.R. Zietlow

*A Bird Begins to Sing: Northwest Poetry
and Prose*
poems from five South Dakota schools
edited by Linda M. Hasselstrom

Library of Congress #78-78375
ISBN 0-917624-11-4

$6.95 paper
$12.95 cloth

Glossary:

A

acetate 39
alterations 40
art 41

B

backbone 43
benday screen 43
bf, bold face 43
bid 43
binders' board 43
binding 43
black-and-white 50
blanket 51
blocking out 51
blow up 52
blueprint 52
blurb 52
bold face type 52
book 53
book paper 53
brayer 53
burnisher 54

C

C 55
© 55
c and sc 55
camera ready copy 55
caption 55
chapbook 55
character 56
cold type 56

Illustrations:

drawings by

Rose Mary Goodson

Appendices:

Who

Anyone with reasonable intelligence and no more than ten thumbs can publish a book. *The Book Book* was begun with schools in mind; the text of a school-produced book would be student writing and students could do all the production tasks, from preparation of the manuscript through construction of several mechanical devices such as light tables. But a single individual who wishes to publish can do everything alone.

Various books on the subject of self-publishing have appeared; many are listed as additional sources of information in Appendix 9. However, many are difficult for the novice to follow, because it's hard to set down a step-by-step pattern in publishing: several processes must occur at once. Some authors assume too much knowledge on the reader's part; some excellent information is scattered among several sources.

Also, many books on the topic begin at page 1 using terms that have not been defined and which are not found in standard dictionaries. I have attempted to correct this problem by *italicizing* words which are likely to be unfamiliar. Italicized words are defined, and sometimes illustrated, in the Glossary. Since you will be learning a new and valuable skill, without benefit of the classroom, approach it as you would any course of study: take notes, read the text, ask questions of former students (printers). That's how I--and about 2500 other small press publishers in the country--learned.

As indicated, the major problem with some sources is the difficulty in arranging the subject in a logical fashion. Therefore, I've used Chapter 1 to discuss the pros and cons of self-publishing. Chapter 2 outlines the whole process, start to finish, showing briefly what choices must be made. In order to fully understand Chapter 2, you must study the lengthy Glossary which defines italicized terms, discusses the background of the choices you will make, and outlines what is required by each choice. Appendices list further sources for specific and detailed information. You will probably collect a number of other references before you finish your book, and you might want to use this one as an encyclopedia in conjunction with one of the step-by-step guides referred to in Appendix 9.

In order to successfully produce your book, study this manual before you begin, and keep it handy as you work. Remember, you're proposing to do something that is a lifework or a job for thousands of people; you must expect to put some effort into it. That I say you can do it is not to minimize the accomplishments of those people who do it as a profession. However, as *The Book Book* demonstrates, you can produce for a few hundred dollars a book that would cost thousands from a royalty publisher--and even more from a vanity press. See Appendix 10 for information on the cost of producing this book.

I've tried to condense much of what I've learned in 15 years of publishing into the following pages, but I must admit that this isn't everything there is to know about publishing. I learned

ii

a lot while researching. It does cover the basic information needed to produce an average book. The way you use that information depends to some extent upon your own powers of observation, your instincts for quality, your personal style, your ability to read and follow instructions.

This book will give you a way to answer the 20 million questions that will assail you in the middle of the night as you begin publishing. I've also consulted most of the sources of information on the subject in print and referred liberally to them in the glossary and various appendices, so you can get additional information if you need it. Don't become a research nut, however, immersing yourself so completely in research that you never produce a book. Because, with this book, a little money and a little patience, you can publish a book. A sense of humor wouldn't hurt.

Where I have quoted or referred often to any particular source, I have given credit; a great deal of information has been made available to hundreds of self-publishers by the real pioneers in the field of our time, including Len Fulton of Dustbooks, Bill Henderson, who published *The Publish-It-Yourself Handbook,* and other members of the Committee of Small Magazine Editors and Publishers (COSMEP).

In addition, in order to test the book in use, I xeroxed copies of the manuscript and used it in a writing and publication project called the "Northwest Outreach" for the South Dakota Arts Council. This project involved my visiting high schools in five towns in northwestern South Dakota (Lemmon, Bison, McLaughlin, Timber Lake and Mc-Intosh), working with the students in writing poetry and fiction, and at the same time producing an anthology of the work written. Both the writing and publication were done in a five-week period, which is a testament to the efficiency of the teachers and students involved, particularly since this was the first writing project they had attempted. Copy was prepared camera-ready by students interested in publication processes and guided through the final steps of printing after the five weeks was over.

I'm also indebted to Jocelyn Hanson, arts coordinator for the South Dakota Arts Council, for handling the details of completing such a complex project in five weeks. And to George Snell, who became my proofreader and husband almost simultaneously.

The National Endowment for the Arts, which has fostered writing and art projects in schools throughout the nation, provided funds through the South Dakota Arts Council to partially pay printing costs. In addition, I received an arts fellowship through SDAC which helped pay some research and writing expenses. Details on production costs are given in Appendix 2.

--Linda M. Hasselstrom
Lame Johnny Press
Hermosa SD 57744

iv

Why

There are a variety of reasons to consider publication of your own book. For one thing, you may have submitted it without success to commercial royalty publishers. I could write several chapters on why they have rejected you, given the biases of major publishers and the poverty of minor ones, but Bill Henderson has already covered the subject; see Appendix 9.

Or you may be a teacher whose students have been doing extensive writing or art you would like to see in book form both for the sake of their pride and the educational opportunities such publication would afford. Many schools have been visited during the past few years by Artists-in-the-Schools/Communities under programs supported by the National Endowment for the Arts through state arts councils. Writing is meant to be read, art to be seen. Therefore, a natural progression of this encouragement of student expression would be to print that work, so students, parents, teachers, administrators and other taxpayers could see what has been accomplished. In many schools, some form of publication has been attempted, usually with the unsatisfactory mimeograph method. While it does reproduce student work, the result is difficult to read and--let's face it--ugly. Good writing deserves attractive printing; poor printing, like sloppy dress on a job applicant, may make the observer think less of the material presented. You may have lamented that there ought to be a better way than mimeograph, but felt that actual publication was financially impossible.

Well, it isn't. In many cases, if you have time and a decent typewriter, you can publish a respectable book for about the same cost as mimeographing. And once you've produced a better-looking book, you may be able to sell it to a built-in audience for enough money to pay for costs of production, plus further programs for the students: more Artists-in-the-Schools/ Communities, more books.

An example is the Northwest Outreach project I mentioned earlier, which in five weeks produced poems for *A Bird Begins to Sing: Northwest Poetry & Prose*. Layout, pasteup and printing took somewhat longer, but the book sold well to those who had been involved in its production, as well as to others in the communities.

When you have a body of good writing, the first question may be, why can't I sell it to a major publisher?

The answer is that big publishers want books that will sell; at least 10,000 copies are required to reach the break-even point. If you have a novel on the order of *Jaws*, put this book down and put the manuscript in the mail to Ballantine. If you have a manuscript of 37 poems, or teach in a small parochial school in Pierre, South Dakota and want to produce a book of grade school students' writing and drawings, don't waste postage. Do it yourself.

Second question: can I get a local printer to handle the job, from handwritten poems to impressive hardbound book, for a reasonable amount of money?

The answer is usually no; I won't attempt
to suggest price estimates, because printer's fees
vary from town to town and month to month. But if
you don't believe me, take the whole bundle down
to a local printer and ask him. If your school, or
you as an individual, can afford it, go ahead.

You'll still find this book helpful in
its sections on copy preparation, negotiating
with printers, and sales. Printers are independent businessmen and generally more crochety than
other small merchants because their product is
mysterious to the public--and yet at any given
moment half the public may want to "get a few
copies of this printed." "This" may range from a
business card to a four-color illustration and
the public wants it yesterday and cheap. Nevertheless, printers are selling a product and it's
to their advantage to cooperate with you--and to
yours to help them by knowing as much as you can
about the requirements of publishing. This book
can help you understand what they do and how to
deal with them more intelligently and more successfully.

Chances are, however, that you will not
be able to afford to have a printer take the rough
copy and turn it into a finished book. What you
need is a compromise, a way to do some of the
work yourself, paying the expert printer to do
only those tasks you cannot do, to keep the cost
reasonable. Since the single greatest expense in
printing is preparation of copy--a step anyone
can do--such a compromise is possible. Chapter 2
discusses in more detail the steps to printing
and the options that are available to you in de-

ciding just how much work you can to toward publication.

Another alternative that is sometimes considered is the vanity publishing house, which
will publishing anything for a price. Many authors
who have unsuccessfully tried the royalty book
publishers turn to vanity publishers, which require that the author pay for publication of his
book. Since that seems to be exactly what I'm proposing, you may ask what the objection is.

The difference is this: a vanity publisher
will seem to offer incentives such as editing,
marketing your book, advertising and review in major publications. But remember, you are not only
paying for the actual publishing (as you do if
you self-publish) you're also paying people to do
work on your manuscript that you can do yourself.
Objective self-editing isn't easy, but you can
probably find an English teacher or critical
friend to help you--and have more editing than a
vanity house would provide.

Advertising and promotion by vanity presses is usually nonexistent or less extensive than
you are led to believe; you can do a much better
job with news releases and personal appearances.
For more on this subject, see Glossary entries on
cooperative publishing, *small presses*, *vanity
publishing* and *promotion*, and references in Appendix 9.

An example of success in self-publishing
is the parochial school I mentioned earlier, St.
Joseph's in Pierre, SD. A young teacher with no
previous experience successfully published a book
of student work, *perfect bound* with paper covers.
Each student wrote and drew his/her own page, sign-

24

ing it with a thumbprint. I visited the school for 3 days to help with publishing plans. The school made enough money through sales of the book, titled *Thumb Prints,* to pay for future Artists-in-Schools/Communities as well as the book's publication costs and my consulting fees. Parents, students and teachers are still benefitting from the book.

I think it's important at this point to make a distinction between "publishing" and "printing". Printing simply means the physical act of producing printed material by means of an inked type and a printing press, or similar method. Publishing is preparing and issuing printed matter for sale or distribution--whether you write and/or print   it or not.

You can be a publisher without being a printer and vice versa. In producing any book, you become a publisher. You might want to take advantage of this fact by choosing a *company name* and *logo* for your press, even if you only plan one book. By so doing, you may take advantages such as wholesale buying or tax breaks from having established a business. The process involves complexities; you should consult an attorney about laws in your area. But costs are low or nonexistent, and advantages outweigh problems.

Besides the practical reasons for publishing a book of your own or someone else's work, there is a more compelling reason: satisfaction. Creating a book is as artistic an endeavor as painting a portrait, though its subtleties are not appreciated by as many people. If the work is your own, of course, there is an extra measure of pleasure in creating the "frame" that will present it to the world, though you

25

doubtless still consider the work of first importance. But if the work is that of someone else and you can be more objective, the pleasure in the creation of the frame in which it is presented may be even more intense. Without that frame, the work might never be seen.

Perhaps the most important answer to the question of this chapter--why?--is because: self-publishing is utterly independent. While no one handles pesky details like where to put page numbers, no one shares the rewards--whether pecuniary or otherwise--of publication. You are The Publisher, and the book is entirely yours.

How

It is difficult to outline a step-by step
process of publishing because several things must
be done simultaneously. You must know, for example,
what sort of book you want before going to a prin-
ter--but printers can help you understand the
choices to be made in defining the book you want.

In addition, it is difficult to explain
those choices without pausing to define each word,
which makes following the steps difficult. My so-
lution to this difficulty is to discuss, chrono-
logically, steps you must follow to produce your
book. Any term with a special definition will be
printed in *italics* so that you can turn to the
Glossary for a more complete definition. If you
are familiar with the meaning, simply ignore the
italics and read on. Be aware, however, that as is
the case with many specialized languages, words in
the printing trade are often the same as words in
the outside world--but with different meanings.
For example, a *signature* is not the name you sign
on your checks, but a group of pages (usually 16)
folded together as part of a book.

Conversely, I have not defined words that
may be unfamiliar but which are defined in any ordinary dictionary. Someone who works on a "free-
lance" basis, for example, is a writer or designer who does not have a regular salary or work for
a single company but offers his/her services in-
dependently.

Also, a checklist is provided in Appendix
1 so that once you begin publication, you can keep

track of the processes you have completed. You might post a copy over your work area, along with the *deadlines* for completion of each item.

First you'll need a schedule. This is particularly evident in a classroom situation, where a limit of nine months may be imposed from writing through publication. But in any job you must set deadlines and stick to them; those deadlines must be made clear to the printer, who may be prone to put you off in favor of jobs involving more money. Constant vigilance over deadlines will be required.

An aid in keeping on schedule is a *flow chart* so that you can know where each portion of the book is at any given time. You should determine, with the aid of your printer, how long each step to publication should take before choosing the final deadline.

The first step to production of any publication after the manuscript has been written and corrected is *copy preparation*, a process including *design* of the *format, layout, typesetting, pasteup* and *art work*.

The second major division is all *presswork, platemaking* and related steps in setting up e-equipment for printing the book, including the press *run, folding* and *collating* or *gathering*.

The third major division in printing is *binding*, and many methods of producing an attractive binding exist.

The special problem for the publisher of a small quantity of books is that costs of setting up printing equipment are prohibitive; for a single printing press to cost $60,000 is not unusual. Since actual printing time is short, however, cost of printing is less than for any other process. The most expensive process is copy preparation. For example, it is cheaper to buy time on an offset press for the brief period necessary to print 1500 48-page books than to buy the time of experienced compositors and layout artists to prepare the copy for the press. I recently received an ad from a company that charges $400 to prepare copy and rough layout for a one-page brochure.

You can buy all the services I've outlined, with enough money; you can do them all yourself, with enough equipment and time. The most practical course is to compromise. I recommend that you plan to do everything except platemaking, printing and binding. If you have extra money after calculating those costs, you might choose to have typesetting professionally done. If you have insufficient money for those operations, you might choose one of several methods of binding by hand.

Defining your book involves, first, selection of the format and determining the book's specifications, or *specs*. The following are the terms with which you must become familiar in order to make these decisions; read each entry in the Glossary and take notes on your preferences as you visualize the book:

> *trim size*
> *page design*
> *page arrangement* (number of pages)
> *paper* (for text and cover)
> *type styles* (for text and headlines)

cover art
cover price

Once you have read each entry, take your
notes and this book, and go to a bookstore or library to examine books similar to the one you
hope to produce. Your goal is to find a balance
between quality and price; no doubt some of the
books you like best will be beyond your price
range or beyond your printer's capabilities.
It's a good idea to choose several books which
appeal to you, take them home and compare them on
the basis of the items in the list. You will begin to see differences in details like page size,
the quality of paper used for the text of the book,
how well cover art reproduces on several types
of cover stock--things you've probably never no-
ticed about books before. This may be the most
important step you do in producing your book,
since most of us, even if we are lovers of reading, tend to ignore the packages in which our
reading material reaches us.

For example, page design, of which we are
rarely aware, influences the readability of a
book a great deal. Where should page numbers be?
Should each poem be centered on the page according to its own width, or should each be set
against a standard margin on the left side of
the page? Where should the author's name appear--
top right? top left? bottom right or left? Centered? If the page is prose, notice now far
apart the lines are on the page; lines of type
with very little white space between them tend
to fade into gray unreadability; see *line spacing.*

There are literally hundreds of choices to be made in your search for the *style* of your book; you must examine some of the alternatives before going to a printer. No doubt you will have to alter some of your choices for cost considerations. I suggest noting several styles that appeal to you for each portion of the forgoing list and studying the books for several days until you can label each of the choices as first, second or third choice.

From these choices, prepare a *dummy*. At this point, it will be only a rough approximation of the final book, but its preparation will help you visualize details, and save your printer dozens of questions.

Then take the dummy, your list of choices and two or three favorite books and make the rounds of local printers, asking if they can provide you with the style of book you prefer and its approximate cost. Since you are not yet a paying customer, the best you can expect is a verbal price estimate or *quotation* rather than a firm, written bid. But besides getting cost information, you'll be gaining valuable knowledge about how printers operate and which will be the most cooperative. Ask for a tour of the facilities, especially noticing whether they have *offset* or *letterpress* systems.

Cooperation and a real desire to help you publish are so important that I would rather work with a friendly printer whose shop is slightly old-fashioned than one with the latest equipment who is not genuinely concerned with helping me produce my book. One simple reason for this is that small printers with older equipment often are not unionized, so that you are allowed to participate more fully in the actual production of your book; one simple reason for its opposite is that the printer with the fancy equipment may have only one thing in mind: paying for his $60,000 press.

While you're talking with the printer, take down unfamiliar terms, and look them up in this book or ask him to explain. Don't be a-fraid to ask questions, to show your ignorance. He'll find out anyway and pretending to know more than you do could be expensive. Also, you can judge a great deal by his willingness to inform you.

Once you've received preliminary cost estimates on each of your various choices for the book, as well as for the entire job, you'll probably go home and rip up all your original plans. It's time for some hard choices.

First, decide what type of copy preparation you prefer and can afford and whether your book will be delivered to the printer *camera ready* or in manuscript form to be *typeset* by the printer.

In addition, select a final page arrangement; do you really need an index? Remember to keep the organization simple and consider the actual needs of the reader of your book. Then estimate the number of pages *(copy measurement)* and prepare a more complete dummy based on your knowledge.

An important part of book preparation often overlooked until the end is cover art and other *illustrations*. It's a good idea to begin work on these along with the body of the book, asking your printer's advice on whether the art you choose will reproduce well on the cover and text paper you have chosen. It's to his advantage to advise you wisely, since he, too, is judged by the resulting book. Cover art requires extra consideration since, assuming you plan to sell the book, it will influence a prospective buyer before the writing inside can; if the cover is amateurishly done, the buyer may never read a line of the work inside. If you have no appropriate illustrative material, note how many attractive covers bear only type arranged imaginatively, or ask the printer about special treatments for photographs.

Since you are by this time reasonably certain you will have a book, study the section on *copyright*, apply for an *International Standard Book Number (ISBN)* and a *Library of Congress Cataloging in Publication* number (if your book is over 50 pages). You can't wait until after typesetting for any of these processes.

You should also produce a *ladder diagram*. This will help you visualize the final product and be essential later when you're working on *layout*.

Next consider the number of copies of the book you intend to publish. Remember that in printing, the greatest cost is in producing the first copy. After the plates are made, each copy produced is cheaper than the one before. For example, it may cost you $3.79 per book to produce 50 books, but at that rate it will cost you only 24¢ per book to produce 10,000 books. However, it's silly to pay for more than you can use, so you also need to calculate the number of copies needed.

Perfect bound books are easier to sell to individuals, because they're cheaper, but if you can manage even 100 hardbound books, your sales to libraries may pay for a substandial portion of your printing costs; see *binding*.

If you plan to give books away, make lists of where they will go until you're sure you have enough--and it's hard to have enough free books--then add 100.

If you plan to sell them, the problem is more complex. *Promotion* methods dictate amount of sales. First calculate the cover price and consider *pre-publication orders*. Once you've decided whether or not to send the book to *reviewers*, and made other decisions listed in the section on promotion, balance enthusiasm with discretion. Keep in mind that personalities also sell books, as do good covers, and low prices. On the other hand, few books produced without a barrage of costly national advertising make any-one rich. Most printers prefer to print in in-crements from 500; ask about *overrun* costs and be modest in your expectations of sales. I rea-lize this paragraph is pretty vague, but no one can advise you on this tricky decision.

After you have thoroughly planned your book, dummied and diagrammed it, calculated costs, determined cover price and promotion me-thods, you'll need to get solid bids from all the printers still under consideration. This is a precise and final step; once you have listed the book's specs, costs will be based on them. Anything you forget and have to add later will be especially, and expensively, charged.

You should write for estimates from printers in other parts of the country as well as local ones. While this may seem unecessary, and while negotiation production by mail may seem risky, it is often the cheapest and best method. There are many excellent low volume (under 10,000 copies) printers in the midwest and south; much of their business comes by mail so they know exactly how to handle the problems. Some of them supply layout and pasteup forms. I've included a list of such printers in Appendix 4. If only for price comparison, you owe it to yourself to write for estimates from several of these. Appendix 2 shows a sample letter of estimate and varied replies. Remember that once you sign the quotation, you have agreed to the printer's conditions--often listed on the back of the agreement. In some cases this requires payment even if you cancel publication, so sign cautiously.

After signing a publication agreement you can begin--officially--actual production. Of course, as I have mentioned, many of these steps overlap; you should have the manuscript prepared by this time, or being typeset, besides having written the Copyright Office, ISBN division and Library of Congress. Cover art should be in process; you should be collecting equipment for pasteup, building a light table, drawing or collecting art--all at once.

Once you've begun typesetting, or delivered your manuscript to the compositor, you must plan layout in detail, with precise measurements and a place for every element that will ap-

35

pear in the book. A mistake in this planning will carry through the entire book.

When typesetting is complete, your printer will return *proofs* for correction. If you're preparing your own copy, on an IBM typewriter for example, xerox the finished sheets so that you need not mark on the original. I've included in the Glossary a list of *proofreader's symbols*, the language that lets you communicate most clearly with your printer. You need not master them if you are preparing your own copy. If you are working with a compositor, go over corrected proofs with extra care; generally an error is corrected by typing an entire line, which allows new errors to be made elsewhere in the line.

When the copy has been proofed, corrected, and proofed again, it's time for pasteup. Careful preparation of the layout should enable anyone to do the subsequent pasteup. However, if you're working with a group of people, it might be easier to have one person responsible for both processes to help insure consistency and accuracy. Remember to have completed pages carefully examined at least once more for error.

After pasteup, the printer will make plates for the book. It's a good idea to insist on examining page proofs made from the completed plates. You should have caught major errors before this time; any changes will require complete dismantling of the page, an expensive process unless the error is clearly the printer's. Nevertheless, this is your last chance to check the accuracy of the book and you should read page proofs carefully.

While the book is being printed, you may

36

do a great deal of promotion. Then printed pages are *collated,* folded, gathered into signatures and bound. Then the book is delivered to the customer (or you might save money by picking it up) and sales can begin. Immediately deposit the required 2 copies with the Copyright Office to complete registration of copyright, and send 1 to the Library of Congress.

If, in reading through these steps to publication once, you consider the process hopelessly confusing, try again, checking each Glossary reference. It can be done; hundreds of people do it every day.

A substantial portion of the impetus to publish comes from attitude. Like most writers, I began by believing that the writing was the end of it all, that my job ended with the final draft neatly typed on clean white paper with ample margins and a minimum of typographical errors. At that point, some mystical person would take over, hand me a fat check, and place a beautiful hardbound book in my hands.

That attitude is similar to the attitude of the woman with a flat tire waiting for a knight in shining armor to ride by with a jack. If you can drive, you can change a tire. And why stand by the side of the road, when with a little effort you could be on your way down the highway? Knowledge, as the gentleman remarked, is power.

ACETATE (rubylith) plastic material used by graphic artists to indicate place-ment of a *halftone*; since red is seen by the camera as black, placing a red acetate window in a page means that when the natative or *flat* is made, a clear window of the same size will ap-pear. The completed halftone negative is then stripped into the flat and *platemaking* proceeds.

Acetate comes in various sizes, colors and degrees of stickiness; for half-tone windows, only red can be used. I suggest Blockout Film by Chartpak, or Para-paque from Bader's (see Appendix 5). Both come in 10" by 14" or 20" by 28" sheets; prices are similar. For the average user, these will serve--though the blockout film, which is backed by paper, tends to shrink in storage and stretch in use. Para-paque is backed by plastic and so remains firmer and easier to measure and cut, but it's more delicate and rips easi-ly. You can send for samples of these and other types of acetate from va-rious companies to decide which you prefer.

When cutting many windows of similar sizes, prepare a layout of those si-zes on your light table, then cut all windows at once. To avoid handling

large sheets of film too much, determine the standard width of most of
your illustrations, and cut off a
strip that width, then cut individual
windows from it. Remember to check
each step with a triangle or T-square
to make sure all angles are square.
Slashes into the acetate window can
often be repaired with invisible tape,
then rubbed over with a red felt tip
marker, rather than cutting a new
window.

Some printers prefer, however, that
you bring all illustrations, including
both *line shots* and *halftones* to the
shop. The printer can then decide which
camera method is appropriate for each
illustration, and can often group them
together (gang them) for copying, saving money and time. Generally, then,
he'll provide you with a *stat* to put
on the *pasteup* for each illustration.

Acetate sheets, also referred to as
color overlay sheets, are useful in
making original art, such as posters,
with a printed appearance that looks
professional without costly multi-
color printing or sloppy and time-
consuming painting. With care and a
plastic or cardboard template, you
can cut acetate to any shape with
clean, crisp lines.

ALTERATIONS (author's alterations): abbreviated
    a.a. for proofreaders; see *typographical
    error.*

ART: any illustration, including arrangement
of type, used to enhance the appearance of a publication; the term also
sometimes refers to finished *pasteup*.
Good art can improve almost any publication; poorly executed work can
mar almost any effort. If you are not
an artist, one source of varied high-
quality items is the Dover Publications Pictorial Archives, a group of
books published for commercial artists, designers, craftsmen, publishers, agencies and others. When
you purchase a book in the PA series,
you buy full reproduction rights to
individual items in the book, without further payment, permission or
acknowledgement. Illustrations are
copyright free and can be used any-
time, any place and in any manner so
long as you do not reproduce the entire book. Many styles are available,
including such things as Renaissance
woodcuts, American Indian designs,
historic designs, old engravings and
catalogs, portraits of famous persons, flora and fauna and innumerable
other items; write Dover Publications,
180 Varick St., NY NY 10014 for more
information.

Other sources of free illustration include material in the public domain--
originally published without copyright, or upon which copyright has ex-
pired. The greatest source of such
materials is old books or magazines.
Also check print collections in lib-

raries, historical societies and museums. These institutions may charge a fee for reproducing the material, but for the quality of the work, the charge is low. Look in secondhand bookstores for old magazines, books or prints. If you need pictures of specific products, businesses producing them are happy to supply you with all the illustrative material you want, as a form of free advertising; contact the public relations department; see Appendix 3 for more sources.

B

BACKBONE: the back of a book; see *binding*.

BENDAY SCREEN: a dot pattern used to produce
a tint of screen effect; while the
term originally referred to a letterpress process, you may now buy a variety of such screens for use in offset; see *illustrations*.

a few of dozens of ben-
day screens available

bf: abbreviation for *boldface type.*

ID: see *quotation*.

BINDERS' BOARD: paper board generally used
in making the cover of a cased or
hardbound book; should be mentioned
in the specifications and *quotation*
or bid returned by the printer; see
binding.

BINDING: refers both to materials (such as
glue and thread) holding a book together with its cover, and to the process
of assembling the finished book, which
includes folding, *gathering*, *collating*, *sewing* or *stitching*, gluing,

trimming, rounding and backing, lining up, casing-in and, finally, putting on the *dust jacket*.

Case (also called hard or cloth) binding, perfect binding and saddle stitching are the most common. In case binding, each *signature* is *smyth sewn* through the middle fold with thread, glued into position on a rigid cover made from cloth-covered binder's board (heavy cardboard).

① sections gathered and sewn

② sections sewn together - then sewn as a whole

③ cover is then glued on

In perfect binding (also called adhesive binding) the folded and collated signatures are trimmed at the back, leaving a rough fiber surface. Wraparound paper covers are glued to this surface. If hardbound books are not possible, this mode of binding is second preference for libraries and booksellers, since the title, author's name and price may be (should be) printed on the *spine*, allowing the book to be displayed and stored in a much smaller area than if the entire cover must be visible. Also referred to as square back binding.

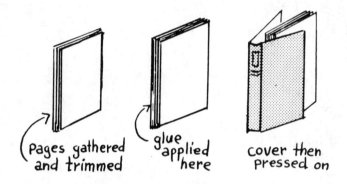

Pages gathered and trimmed

glue applied here

cover then pressed on

Saddle-stitching is the simplest form of permanent binding, with 2 or 3 wire staples punched through the middle of the single crease; sometimes called pamphlet binding.

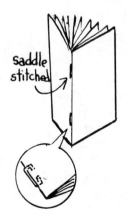

saddle stitched

Some books are also side-stitched
with wire staples; the spine is
creased and folded to form a square
back, then wire staples are punched
through the cover and text pages from
front to back; not attractive, and
not very durable.

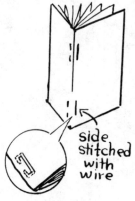

side
stitched
with
wire

Spiral binding is coming into use for
workbooks, cookbooks and similar publications; spirals are available in
plastic and metal. If they appeal to
you, check prices locally and then
check catalogs to compare mail order prices. Remember, not every printer can apply the spirals, though for
a short run, some can be applied
by hand.

If you have few pages and only a few
books, you might consider hand binding. Consult Appendix 3 for sources
on its complexities; the sketch shows
a simple method that is attractive,
fast, and quite durable. The threa-
ded needle is pushed through the fol-

ded book, starting at the center of
the inside fold, then back through
the fold nearer one end. Stretch the
thread down the inside fold to a
point near the other end, push out,
back through near the center and tie
across the long thread running down
the center fold. Leave at least a
half inch end and tie a tidy knot.
For speed, you might want to pre-
punch holes. Any strong thread will
do, though some binders prefer linen,
available in printing supply houses.

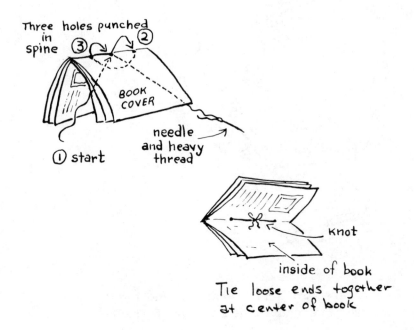

Three holes punched in spine

③ ②

BOOK COVER

needle and heavy thread

① start

knot

inside of book

Tie loose ends together at center of book

I've also seen books printed on separate sheets, then boxed instead of
bound; in one case the sheets ap-

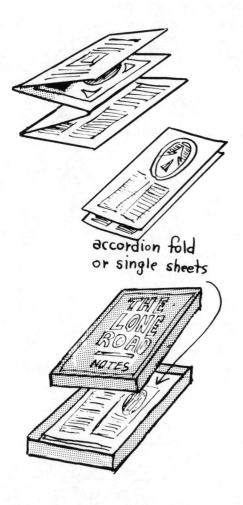

accordion fold
or single sheets

peared in a flat box, in another
they were arranged recipe fashion

(*Wing Span of an Albatross*, poems
by Rochelle Holt's Ragnarok Press)
as shown in the sketch. See *The*

Boxed book

Shoestring Publisher's Guide and
Bookbinding for Beginners, and various
references on binding, Appendix 9).

Another term you may encounter is library binding, which refers to specially reinforced bindings for library use. Some publishers bind special library editions, but you need not go to that expense.

If you can afford case binding on even 100 copies of your book, sales to libraries will increase; when buying softbound books, libraries often have to buy duplicate copies, or take into consideration costs for rebinding the books, and they have tended to avoid books from small presses for this reason.

When discussing binding with your printer, ask if he does his own or sends the books out; if the latter, you can sometimes save money by having the bindery ship the finished books directly to you instead of back to the printer, who then ships them on to you at your expense.

BLACK AND WHITE: originals or reproductions in black ink on white paper, or any single color ink on single color paper, as distinguished from *multi-color* or *four-color process*. While color is attractive, it is out of reach financially for most self-printers and requires technical equipment not found in most small printing shops, as well as multiple press runs. Dramatic effects can be achieved with black and white reproduction; see *illustrations*.

BLANKET: see *offset lithography*.

BLEED: extending printed image to edge of
the paper, eliminating all unprinted margins. An illustration of any
kind can be *scaled* to bleed top,
bottom, left, right, or on all 4
sides; you must allow for 1/8 to
1/4 inch to be trimmed from the
illustration without damaging the
intent; very effective, but should
be a consistent part of the book's
style rather than an isolated item.

May also refer to an unwanted stain
or fuzziness in offset printing,
especially in color.

bleed

BLOCKING OUT: eliminating undesirable back-
grounds such as portions of a negative
by *opaquing*; the term sometimes refers

to covering blotches or smudges on
the negative resulting from careless-
ness in pasteup; generally costs extra, since it is a time-consuming
process.

BLOW UP: to enlarge photographically.

BLUEPRINT (blues): in offset lithography and
photoengraving, a photographic print
made from the entire page after it has
been stripped up; reproduced in either negative or positive, it is
used as a proof to check position
of the elements of the page; sometimes referred to as book blues.

BLURB: description of the book's contents,
possibly with review comment, printed
on the front and/or back flaps or
on the back of the book jacket.

BODY TYPE: type used for the bulk or body of
book; text type, distinguishde from
headline or display type, boldface
or italics; see *type style*.

BOLD FACE TYPE: Heavier than text type, but
of the same face; see *type face* and
example below.

ɔt-long yellow rectangle.
planes that occasionally
dirt! Wet the cactuses

BOOK: is, according to UNESCO, a "non-periodi-
cal literary publication containing
49 or more pages, not counting covers"; the U.S. Postal Service requires that a book mailed by book
rate have 24 pages or more, of which
at least 22 are printed, with no ad-
vertisements. These restrictions are
not important if you do not plan to
deal with either UNESCO or the USPS.

BOOK PAPER (body paper): used for the pages of
the book, as distinguished from cover
paper; see *paper*.

BRAYER: a roller used in art and pasteup; see
pasteup tools.

BURNISHER: a plastic or plastic-tipped tool similar to a cuticle stick, used to apply rubbing pressure to transfer type to make it adhere to the page; attempting to burnish (or rub down) press-type with a sharp point such as a pencil or ballpoint pen will damage the acetate backing. The burnisher, or any similar rounded surface such as the bowl of a spoon or the rounded reverse ends of some pens, can give correct pressure and insure that the type is bonded to the pasteup surface.

C

C: standard printer's abbreviation for 100, as "4C copies"; always capitalized.

©: symbol for copyright; may be hand drawn; used in conjunction with the name of the copyright claimant and year of publication; see *copyright*.

c and sc: caps and small capitals; to indicate that copy should be set in this manner: ORATOR

Not all typesetting equipment is capable of setting c and sc.

CAMERA READY COPY: full text of book--type art, drawings--pasted up in final form and ready to be photographed for production without further work on the part of the platemaker; abbreviated as crc.

CAPTION: copy written to explain illustration or photograph; technically refers to the title appearing above an illustration, as contrasted with *legend* which usually appears below; in actual practice the term refers to matter appearing in either location or beside the illustration.

CHAPBOOK: originally a cheap book, paperbound, popular in 17th and 18th Century England and America; now often used by

small presses to indicate similar
books produced inexpensively, often
in a series, presenting the work of
young poets for the first time.

CHARACTER: a single letter; the term is
often used in measurements, as "12
characters per inch."

COLD TYPE: copy created by computer typesetting device or typewriter for use
in *offset* printing, as opposed to
hot type, which is molten lead cast
into lines of type for *letterpress*
printing.

COLLATE: assembly of single sheets (pages)
into complete sets--all the pages in
the book--prior to folding, *gathering*
and *binding*; time-consuming if done by
hand. Ask your printer about charges;
if they're minimal, it's faster to
have him do it. But if he's hand-col-
lating, or using slow equipment, and/or
if you are working with students, you
might save money and learn by doing it
yourself.

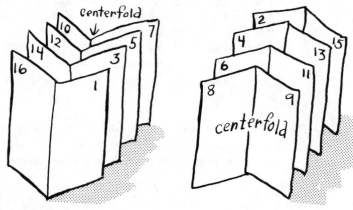

COLOPHON: brief statement at the end of a book giving facts pertaining to its publication, such as the book's designer, type styles used, the printer, paper. This is a traditional touch, not essential; it is reappearing with the spread of small publishers devoted to production of beautiful books.

COLOR: probably because we see it so much, color fascinates us, and almost every novice publisher hopes to have more than "plain" black and white in his first publication. But even one color adds considerably to costs, and it seems to me that some very impressive substitutes for color can be found in unique or large types, in *art*, in *benday screens*, or in *design*. Before considering color, read the *illustration* and *design* entries in the Glossary, and examine some books that have eye appeal without additional color. If you still want color, consider using a tinted paper and a single-colored ink; many printers will charge very little more than for black on white, as long as you still have only one color ink on one color paper. The reason for the extra cost lies in the expense and time of *wash-up*.

Adding a second color--and before you even consider this check the cost with your printer--is relatively simple. Paste up the *job* as if it were to be

in one color only. Then tape a thin
tracing sheet over the work and mark
the areas to be printed in color. The

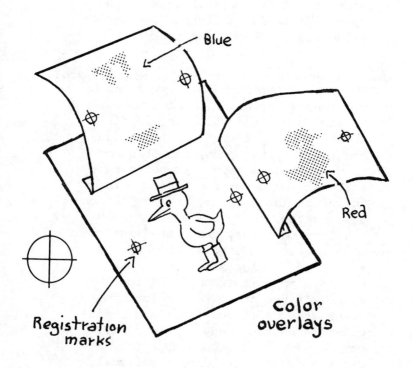

camera man makes one negative, then
masks it so that only the first color
shows. When the plate of the first color is complete, he masks that and ex-
poses the second color. Colors can
be added almost indefinitely by this

method, so long as you keep adding tissue overlays and keeping each color separate. Note that each tissue overlay is keyed in place by the use of identical registration marks; that is, the symbol at left (which can be purchased with press-type lettering or drawn by hand) is placed on the same location, well outside the print area, on each layer that the printer will work with. This insures that when the elements of the finished illustration are put together, they will *register* correctly, or be lined up as they should be.

Or, if you prefer not to work in such detail with the overlays, simply trace the outline of the material to be printed in a second color roughly on the tissue and let the printer do the fine work--at an extra charge.

A number of the general references listed in Appendix 9 have sections explaining the process involved in color work in more detail; I think the best are in *Pocket Pal* and *Bookmaking*; see also *four-color process* in this Glossary.

COMPANY NAME: a name under which you operate as publisher, separate from whatever other business or private interests you may have; can "legitimize" your business in the eyes of other businesses, making it easier for you to get attention and credit from printers, and deal with book-

stores and booksellers. A company name
instantly creates an impression of
serious purpose, helps you avoid the
stigma that sometimes clings to "self-
publishing"; and some firms, such as
paper companies and printers will reply
to your letters only if they are on company stationery. In choosing a name under
which to operate, your own imagination is
your only limit--and names already in
use. Check the *International Directory
of Little Magazines and Small Presses*
(Appendix 9) for names already in use.
Then pick a type style that seems to suit
the style of the name, and which will always be used in conjunction with the company name. Selection of a *logo* is another
part of choosing a name, but a logo is not
essential. If you decide to use one, you
might find ideas in the Dover Pictorial
Archives series of books (Appendix 3). Or
talk to an artist about your idea of a
symbol for the name you've chosen or the
type of publishing you plan to do. Or let
the typeface, arranged in some distinctive
manner, be the only logo of the company.

Once you've chosen a name and established
some symbolic form, you'll need a permanent address--even a post office box which
can remain constant. Then you need to
check the laws in your area to determine
how to begin to operate legally as a company. In most areas, this is simply a matter of filing with the County Clerk a
statement that you are doing business under the company name you've picked. Sometimes you must pay a small fee, or pub-

licize the company name; to discover what the requirements are in your area, call the Chamber of Commerce or the County Clerk. Do all of this early in your publishing venture, even if you only print one book--because later explanations to various bureaucracies are more difficult.

Once you've established the company name, filled in the proper forms in triplicate, order some statinery printed at the local quick-print. In my opinion, letterhead stationery is the most important, though company envelopes are impressive as well. (I save money by using them only for early contacts with customers, and with other businesses, and using plain white ones for other kinds of business--applying the return address with a rubber stamp). Invoices imprinted with the company name are also important for contact with stores, but business cards may or may not be to your liking. Take time to design the stationery--considering in what position the name and address should appear, choosing a paper with some weight and distinction. Remember that this stationery will often be the first impression others will have of you and your work, and it can create a favorable or unfavorable idea. Consider varying the placement of the address: some businesses place it vertically at the left of the envelope, or at the bottom of the stationery instead of at the top. And always include the telephone number, if you have one.

Composition: see *typesetting*.

CONSIGNMENT: an agreement to leave books at
a store, which agrees to pay after the
books sell, deducting 40% of the *cover
price* for the store's trouble. I'd prefer not to leave books on consighment,
to insist bookstores buy them on the
spot to reduce my time and trouble. I
always discuss the sale on this assumption. Occasionally, a bookstore with a
shoestring budget will say they simply
can't afford to buy, so I'll consign.
Other bookstores sometimes refuse to buy,
and if it seems important to me that the
book be available there, I will consign.
You'll have to judge for yourself on individual cases. Many authorities, such as
Richard Morris, who's worked with COSMEP
for 15 years, discourages small press
publishers from consigning at all. If
you do persuade the store to buy copies,
you might do so partly by reminding them
that you'll accept *returns* for credit--
unsold copies in good condition can be
returned for cash refund. Or give the
store a substantial *discount*--perhaps
50%--for buying instead of asking consignment. If you do consign, keep careful records, recording all payments,
books sold, discount, dates, and make
sure the store has a duplicate of your
record. You'll find some stores that
argue with your figures, insisting that
they didn't sell 6 books. You'll have to
decide whether that kind of business is
worthwhile.

A sample form for consigning books
might look like this:

```
Store:          Poet's Bookstore
Address:        111 Smith St.
                Fairburn, SD 57730


From:           Lame Johnny Press
                Box 66
                Hermosa SD 57744

Date:           July 15, 1978

Consigned:      40%

Paid:           _____

Due:            _____
```

Quantity	Title	Price	Total
10	*Homemade Poems*	$3	$30.00
	less 40% ($1.20/book)		
	Total due: ($1.80/book)		$18.00

You can type forms or have them printed at the *quick-print* shop, or purchase similar forms at a supply store.
Then you may keep a running account
of amounts paid and the total due in
the spaces supplied. See *promotion*.

C ONVERSION WHEEL: see *scaling wheel*.

C OOPERATIVE PUBLISHING: involves shared
        ownership and shared responsibility
        for books produced, though forms of
        cooperation among members of coops

vary. Some are work cooperatives, in which you participate in *layout, pasteup,* printing, sales and *promotion* of your own book--and other books produced by the cooperative. Others involve shared payment for various jobs. Many cooperative presses have a single objective; Alice James Books, for example, publishes only quality books of poetry primarily by women. If you feel that self-publishing is simply too complex, especially for a first book, you might want to check on any cooperatives in your area, to learn through working with experienced publishers. The best source I've seen on the whole subject of cooperative printing is Michael Scott Cain's *The Co-Op Publishing Handbook* (Appendix 9). It is likely that because of the decline of quality in books produced by the major publishers, cooperative publishers and other small presses will increasingly attract the attention of the reading public and may even, in some far distant day, manage to make a profit! Small presses and self-publishers have historically produced some of the finest books in the world. Other cooperative and small presses are listed in *The International Directory of Little Magazines and Small Presses* (Appendix 9).

COPY: all material--typed manuscript, art, and

heads--to be used in the production of a book or other printed matter; *Copyreading* is correction of this matter, by the use of *copyreader's symbols*; see also *proofs*.

C OPY MEASUREMENT: is complex; printers with 20 years' experience often disagree on the length that a manuscript will be after it is *typeset*. If a printer is doing your typesetting, let him estimate how long the finished book will be. Type books available to printers list the characters-per-pica of the most common *type faces* and a printer has only to refer to the proper chart. If you're doing your own typesetting, just type the finished copy of the manuscript before determining the number of pages in the book. If you demand precision, *Pocket Pal* (Appendix 9) has one method of copy measurement. And Bader's (Appendix 5) sells an inexpensive copy caster for figuring length in more than 8000 *fonts* and 800 type faces, as well as a character counter scaled for both pica and elite typewriter sizes.

C OPY PREPARATION: steps to produce *camera ready copy* from a manuscript, including *manuscript preparation, copyreading, typesetting* and *pasteup,* the most expensive part of the publication process if you are buying someone else's time.

65

Copy may simply be typed neatly on good quality white paper with the cleanest typewriter and newest ribbon you can find. Copy prepared this way can be taken to an *offset* printer for *reproduction*. The resulting pages will be identical to the typed copy in every detail since the printer simply photographs the pages you have typed.

Another variation on this method is to type copy in good form, then *justify* it, a process which results in the even margins we have come to associate with professionally-printed books. Anyone who can type can justify and the book's appearance will be more professional even if the copy is typewritten.

The ultimate in these simple approaches is to use a carbon ribbon typewriter for its sharp lettering, preferably the correcting model to help keep copy clean, with copy either justified or unjustified. The latter is the method chosen for this book. Copy is being prepared on an IBM Correcting Selectric II without justification.

All of these methods of copy preparation can be done without any outside help at all, if you have the typewriter. If not, you can rent or buy one, or hire a typist, and still spend less than for commercial typesetting.

Commercial typesetting is expensive
but copy prepared in this way is automatically justified, clean, sharp and
readable with a more professional look
than the best image produced by a
typewriter. In addition, you may
choose from a variety of *type faces*
to help set a definite *style* for your
book. The process may be expensive; at
the time I bought my typewriter, commercial typesetting in my area was $15
per book page. At that rate, I paid for
my $795 typewriter with 53 pages of
typesetting.

COPYREADER'S SYMBOLS: used to correct manuscript copy, as opposed to *proofreader's symbols*, these are a universal
language understood by printers everywhere; by using them you may be more
sure of making your exact instructions
clear to the compositor. If you are
preparing your own copy from your own
manuscript, it is not necessary to
master these symbols.

Instruction	Example and Symbol
paragraph	⌐John Frank, president
do not paragraph	No ℂ𝓗 John Frank, president
insert word	today Dr. Munson⌃met with
insert letter	Dr. Munson met today with t⌃e

delete word and close up space	Borglum was ~~very~~ sure
delete letter, close up space	The pro̶cess has begun
close up space	Henry had fi⌣ve of the loveliest
transpose words	The girl rapidly trotted
transpose letters	Frank gallantly tried
delete words and connect	a shellac-like spray used to pro-
	tect a finished drawing; ~~spray fin-~~
	~~ishes are available.~~ If you're care-
separate words	protect⫽finished
insert quotation marks	He said," hogwash"
delete word, insert correct spelling	The ~~Fixitive~~ fixative is

68

insert hyphen	The half‿life
insert dash	Yes‿but will it play
insert period	It was snowing⊙
insert comma	The girl, about ten‿came
insert apostrophe	Its a good question
indent entire paragraph	The special problem for the pub-lisher of a small quantity of books is that costs of copy pre-
make it upper case	The chief said
make it lower case	The Chiefs of three
set in italics	The Gray Goose
set in bold face	The author, Jane Smith
set in small caps	Hermosa. This morning
abbreviate	842 North Podunk Avenue

spell out	842 Ⓝ Podunk Ⓐⓥⓔ
put into figures	I counted (two hundred)
spell out	He was (85)
more follows (when placed at bottom of page)	*more*
end of copy (when placed at end of manuscript)	(#)
restore deleted word	(Stet) It is ~~nevertheless~~ time

COPYRIGHT: is not hard to do, though it may
be difficult to understand; for a text of
the new law and additional helpful explanations, write to the Copyright Office, Register of Copyrights, Washington D.C. 20599. Basically, copyright
protects your right to print, reprint
and copy your work; the right to sell
and distribute copies of the work; the
right to revise, translate or set it
to music as well as other *rights*. It
adds prestige and protects the work
from being reprinted without your permission. The act of publication with
notice secures copyright; if copies

are printed without the notice, the
right to secure copyright is lost.

A book's author claims copyright; if
there are a number of authors, as in
the case of students in a school, the
school may hold copyright in the name
of the children. Three steps must be
taken to copyright a work:

1. produce the copies with copyright
notice in the proper form and position. The copyright notice consists
of three elements: (a) the word "Copyright" and/or the symbol © ; (b) the
year of publication, which is the year
copies were first placed on sale or
distributed; (c) the name of the
copyright owner or owners. Example:
Copyright 1975 George Jones. The 3
elements should appear together, in
that order, on all copies; that is,
they must be printed at the same time
as the other elements of the book;
the notice should appear on the title
page or the page immediately following;

2. publish the work, that is, print
and distribute the work;

3. register the claim in the Copyright Office; this is done by sending,
immediately after publication, 2
copies of the work, a properly completed and notarized Application for
Registration (obtainable from your
printer or from the Copyright Office)
and a $10 check, money order or bank

draft made payable to the Register of Copyrights. Do not send cash. Mail the 3 items in a single package to the address above.

CORRECTIONS: while it may be possible to paint over an error with Liquid Paper or the other opaque white inks, and retype the mistake correctly, this frequently produces a shadow effect that will mar the finished book. I prefer to retype the entire line in which the mistake appears, then tape it over the original line containing the mistake. By leaving the line in place, you can (using the light table) line up the corrected line precisely. This adds a little thickness, but in most cases will not be a problem in the finished copy. An example of this type of correction is the first line of this paragraph. If you want perfection, you can cut out the incorrect line--very carefully--tape it to the light table, place the corrected line under it and cut around the original so that the corrected line is exactly the same shape, then tape the correction back into the hole left in the copy. However, this takes practice--during which you may slash fingers and other copy--and is generally not necessary.

COVER ART: refers to anything on book's cover, whether it is simply the title of the book and the author's name, or an illustration, or type elements arranged in some manner. See *design*.

72

In giving instructions to your printer, "Covers 1 and 4" refers to the two outside sheets; "Covers 2 and 3" to the faces of the cover that are inside. Covers 1 and 4 are usually *varnished* to increase durability.

Following are some examples of cover art, so that you may compare for effectiveness.

The wood or linoleum cut on this cover makes a striking design, but I find the cover unsatisfying because it gives little information about the contents. (Abraxas Press)

A COUNTRY FOR OLD MEN

And Other Stories

E. R. ZIETLOW

This cover uses a dropout halftone
(see *illustration*); the tractor image
wraps around the book, so the rear
wheels are on the back of the *jacket*.
(Lame Johnny Press)

TRUCK 17

$3.00

A simple but strong cover from Truck
Press.

THE
B
O
O
BOOK:

A
Publishing Manual
for Beginners
and Others

THE
BOOK:
BOOK:

A
Publishing
Handbook

The Book
Book:

A Manual
for Beginners
and Others

THE

BOOK

BOOK

L. Hasselstrom

Here are four *thumbnails* of designs I
considered for *The Book Book* when I
first began writing it.

COVER PRICE (sale price, list price): price at which you choose to sell the book. It should be high enough to pay for your time and work (if you consider that important), all production costs (materials, *press-type*, *stats*, *art*, tools, equipment, everything) printing and *promotion* costs (including telephone calls, stamps, paper, scotch tape, etcetera etcetera). To figure how much each book will have cost by the time you hold it in your hand, make generous estimates for each of these items and add them to the printing *estimate* as soon as you receive it; then add about a third of the final figure to allow for items you have forgotten and divide by the number of books you intend to print.

Then remember that any bookstore or other distributors who handle your book will want at least 50% of the cover price. If you plan to distribute the book by mail, keep in mind ever rising postal costs. (When I prepared the first draft of this book, the first pound of books could be sent for 30¢; as I copyread that draft, the cost had risen to 48¢, or a 60% rise in two months; another raise is scheduled for July, 1979, to 59¢). Also, you may decide to use a different class of mail at a higher rate since the USPS has a serious problem in delivering intact anything but first class and insured mail. A large part of my postal costs involve replacing books that do not reach their destination. So

77

make a generous allowance based on
current postal costs, then double it.

In addition, allow for time consumed
in filling out invoices in triplicate
or quadruplicate for libraries and
schools; in addressing and wrapping
packages; in buying properly padded
book shipping bags, strapping tape and
other essentials.

A good rule, then, is to add all the
costs you can imagine, then multiply
by four or five to arrive at the book's
cover price. If this seems too commercial, remember that many self or
small publishers have found themselves
actually losing money on each book
mailed out because they did not allow
enough.

Of course you must also try to decide
how high you can raise the price without losing the particular class of
people your book should appeal to. If
you expect to make a profit, it too
must be reflected in the cover price.
And remember, psychologically it's
better to charge $4.95 than $5.

When you have arrived at a price that
seems satisfactory to you, compare it
with the prices for books of comparable
size, binding and subject matter. Chances are any book priced similarly was
produced by another small press; books
by major companies are often even more

expensive. According to *Publishers Weekly,* the average price of a hardcover book in 1974 was $14.09, and of a paperback $4.38.

COVER STOCK: see *paper.*

CREDIT LINE: line of print with source of photograph, illustration, map, or to the source of other information; sometimes printed below or at the side of the items; sometimes credits are included among other acknowledgements in the front of the book.

CROP: delete unwanted *copy,* usually on a photograph or *illustration.* It is not necessary to use all of a given photo; much better effects may often be achieved by cropping down to the portion of the photo that best illustrates your point. By the use of a compass or various *templates,* you can crop a photo or drawing in shapes other than the usual square or rectangle. You might even trace the shapes that you wish to retain in the photograph onto a sheet of paper and tape it over the photo, as shown in the sketch, to create a silhouette or other effect; see *crop marks, scaling.*

CROP MARKS: on margins of drawings or photographs, indicating which areas are to be removed, to serve as a guide to the cameraman; marks should always be made in pairs to determine a straight line, and should appear outside the printing area. That is, if you're de-

leting only a portion of the photograph at the top, you should place
crop marks at both top right and top
left, as indicated in the sketch; keep
them straight and the photo square by
using your triangle in marking. Even
if the photo is expendable, don't cut
it--you may decide later to change the
size or shape. Or you may want to use
the photo for another purpose, such as
in *promotion*. Also remember to key the
photo to its location in the *layout* by
identifying it on the back as "photo
a, p.23" and perhaps adding its size
and your press name as well. Do not
write on the backs of photos with pen
or pencil, since the sharp point will

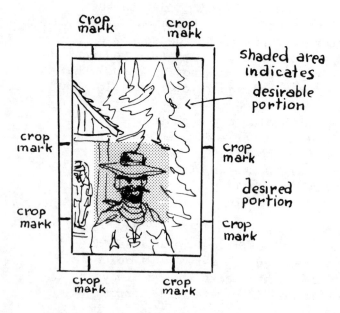

damage the emulsion; grease pencil can smudge. A felt tip pen works well, or you might type information on a stick-on label. If the photo is an only copy, crop marks can be made on a tissue *overlay* (like the one in the sketch on *color*. On illustrations, use an *NRB pencil* to indicate crop marks.

CROSS SECTION PAPER: see *layout paper*.

CURSIVE TYPE: see *type style*.

CUSTOMER CHANGES: see *typographical error*.

CUT: in *letterpress*, engraving or illustration of any kind; sometimes used to refer to the original photograph.

D

DEADLINE: date when a process must be completed in order for the publication to stay on schedule and be finished in time; your printer may give you certain deadlines and your own schedule should allow for a few extra days. In working with young people I always keep the printer's deadlines secret, and set working deadlines 5 to 10 days ahead of those required by the printer to leave time for disaster.

DECORATIVE TYPE: see *type style*.

DELETE: strike out, remove, order removed; see *copyreader's* and *proofreader's symbols*.

DESIGN: the way the book's elements— *type faces, cover art, page arrangement, art,* even page numbers—combine to create an appealing look; the single element that is most likely to reveal that you've self-published your book. Two reasons exist: most of us aren't aware of well-designed books because good design enhances the contents rather than drawing attention to itself, and most self-publishers try to save money in ways that lead to poor design.

First, look at sources in Appendix 9 for information on design; I've had no design courses so have tried particularly to find information on this subject. Much of the material is scattered and vague and you'll have to rely on your own instincts. Go to your local bookstore and/or library and pick out books that appeal to you, then dissect why they do. Try to stick to black and white books, if that's what your budget allows. It's easy for a four-color picture of a peacock on a cover to catch a potential reader's eye; how do you do that using only the title? Even if you can't draw, sketch various possibilities. You'll notice all sorts of gimmicky ways to arrange the author's name and title; keep in mind the importance of readability.

But design involves more than the cover; notice the readability of *body type* and *headline types*, and the way the book designer has combined different *type faces* that seem to belong together. Notice the width of margins; novices often try to cram more type onto each page to save money, reducing readability and creating a less appealing book. Note *line spacing,* another area where self-publishers often try to cheat their budgets. Notice how pleasing black type is; gray type is unreadable, ugly.

Soon you'll begin to see differences between professionally designed books with readable types, uniform paper colors, crisp cover designs, and books designed by amateurs. Then try to imitate the professionals.

If you must save money, do it by preparing your own *camera ready copy* or by typing your work on an IBM typewriter rather than having a *typesetter* do it. Be strict about certain things: select a printer who can give you good black type, rather than using *quick-print* because it's cheaper; choose *paper* that has good texture and finish (rather than the thinnest because it's cheap or the thickest vellum); learn how to use *press-type* rather than pay high prices for type set by printers. A little research will show you that there are many books with beautiful, appealing covers, readable text pages, good *bindings*-- designed and printed on less than a shoestring budget. You might order a few books from some publishers in the *Small Press Record of Books* (Appendix 9) or small press distributors (Appendix 6) to study; many small publishers give pertinent information in the *colophon* or would be happy to tell you how they produced certain effects if you write to them and enclose a self-addressed, stamped envelope (SASE) for a reply. Also look for some of the titles listed in Appendix 9: *Bookmaking*, *Design with Type*, *Editing by Design*, *Graphics Handbook*, *Publish-It-Yourself Handbook*.

Dɪsᴄᴏᴜɴᴛ: distributors and bookstores take a percentage of the *cover price*, phrasing it in this way, "40% discount." This means if your book is cover priced at $4.95, you send or take it to the store, which pays you $2.97 on each book sold (or $1.98--40%--less than the cover price). You pay postage and shipping costs. Standard discounts are 40% to bookstores, 50 to 60% to wholesale distributors and jobbers, and 25% to libraries. Some small bookstores operate on the SCOP (Single Copy Order Plan) under which they send you a check with their order, arbitrarily deducting 1/3 of the cover price of the book. It would cost you more to inform the bookstore that you don't give discounts than you lose on the sale; I suggest filling the order and sending along a polite note indicating the price of the book for future orders.

Bookstores and distributors won't handle your books without this discount, so it must be included in your cover price. Book jobbers (which order books for libraries and other institutions) will ask for a similar discount. Many publishers don't give library discounts and it seems to be unecessary.
You might want to print an information sheet listing discounts and terms of payment to send to prospective distributors; if it's printed on a postcard, all you have to do is address and stamp it. A sample card might read:

"Due to the high cost of bookkeeping and billing on small orders, we require payment in full with order. Books in saleable condition may be returned for credit not less than 90 days nor more than 12 months after date of publisher's invoice. If books are returned with a copy of the invoice, 100% of the invoice price, minus postage, will be credited. Otherwise it will be assumed that there was no original discount. No discount is allowed unless accounts are paid within 30 days. Bookstores and distributors 40% discount; orders of 50 or more books, 50% discount."

The higher discount might induce purchase of books in greater volume, but this might also result in greater returns so it may be unnecessary.

DISPLAY TYPE: see *type style*.

DISTRIBUTORS: see *discount*.

DUMMY: can refer to rough preliminary sketch of a book and to a more complex preview using *proofs* pasted into page forms. It's a good idea to "dummy up" the book in rough form early in planning; count out half the number of sheets expected in the book, fold in half and staple at the center; then number pages and roughly draw in the material for each page. While this doesn't give an idea of length, it can clarify your mental picture of the book's *illustrations*, reveal where you've juxtaposed matter that doesn't belong together and point up other problems.

Early in your discussions with the printer, find out if he wants *pasteup* on single sheets or two sheets at a time. If the latter, care must be taken to get sheets in the proper page order, since the first *sheet* is also the last, and contains four *pages*. For example, a booklet of 12 pages contains 3 printed sheets and 6 *pasteup* sheets:

Sheet #1:   pages 12 and 1, 2 and 11

Sheet #2:   pages 10 and 3, 4 and 9

Sheet #3:   pages 8 and 5, 6 and 7

Let me reiterate, discuss this with

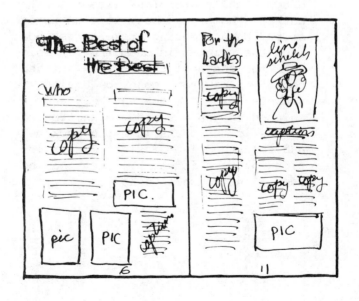

your printer before pasteup; it is much easier to use single sheets and let the printer worry about putting them together correctly. In that case, however, be sure to check order of pages in your final proofing session. Another helpful method is to use a *ladder diagram*.

DUOTONE: process for reproducing an illustration in 2 colors from a black and white original; cheaper than four-color reproduction, but more interesting than a black and white.

DUST JACKET (jacket): printed paper cover wrapped around case bound books both to protect them and for decorative and informational purposes, since case *bindings* usually are blank except for the author's name and book title on the *spine*. When ordering jackets, ask how much the printer is charging for folding them and applying to the finished book; you may save money by having the jackets folded on one end only and shipped to you with the books. You can then slip the books into the jackets and fold the flaps inside. See *promotion* for ways in which jackets may be used alone to sell books.

E

END PAPER: see *binding*.

ENGRAVING: term applied to any printing
plate, generally zinc, made by applying an acid bath, which etches the desired *illustration* deeply enough so it
will hold and transter ink when placed
on the press; used in *letterpress
printing*.

ESTIMATE: see *quotation*.

EXACTO KNIFE: see *x-acto knife*.

FACE: printing surface of a piece of type; *type face* refers to style or design of type.

FIXATIVE: a shellac-like spray used to protect finished drawing or *pasteup* from smudges; if you're careful, and perhaps a bit lucky, fixative is not necessary. Spray the fix lightly or it may cause ink to run.

FLAT: in *offset,* assembled negatives or positives, ready for *platemaking.* The flat is placed over an aluminum plate, which is exposed to light, and burns the impression of the page into the emulsion on the plate--just as images from a photographic negative are burned into photographic paper. The areas on the plate that are struck by light will carry the ink during the printing process. Once the book is printed, plates are discarded, but flats are kept on file in case you wish to order a second printing. Since flats are already prepared, expenses will be lower to reprint than for original printing. Some printers may contact you after a specified period of time to see if you wish to have your flats shipped back to you, or destroyed. In all cases, have them returned, and store them flat if possible (or rolled if that's how they're shipped) in a cool, dry place. They'll keep for years and you never know when you might want to reprint.

FLOP: see *reverse*.

FLOW CHART: helps organize the book's elements, especially if several authors are involved; list each process to be completed and the separate components of the book, then check when each phase is completed. See Appendix 1.

FLUSH: indicates absence of indentation; flush left means each line begins at left margin, as in the copy you are reading; flush right indicates that elements are even at a right margin; you may want *heads* to line up flush left or right with the ends of lines in poetry, for example. Conversely, ragged right or left indicates copy is not even; the copy you are reading is set ragged right.

F.O.B.: used in *quotations* to indicate that customer pays all shipping charges; literally "free on board."

FOLIO: page number

FONT: an alphabet in *upper* and *lower case* for a given style and size of type. If your printer says, "That's a nice type but I don't have a full font of it," you may still be able to use it for *heads* if you don't need the missing letters.

FORMAT: appearance of a book, determined by its *specifications*.

FOTOTYPE: *cold type* method of setting copy, involving letters printed on sheets of white paper backed with adhesive; letters are peeled off the adhesive and aligned in a composing stick, which is marked for measurement. The completed headline is then removed from the stick and placed on the pasteup. A distinct advantage to foto-type over *presstype* is its self-aligning, self-spacing feature, eliminating the need to "eyeball" spacing. The composing stick is a necessary tool, however, and costs around $11, which presstype requires only a burnisher or the end of a pen.

To find out which you prefer, write for a free catalog, which includes a sample of type; if you're interested, the company offers a 30-day trial offer without obligation to buy. The address is Fototype, Inc., 1414 Roscoe St., Chicago IL 60657.

FOUR-COLOR PROCESS (printing): enables a printer to reproduce an infinite range of colors through the use of black and variations of the primary colors of red, blue and yellow, on white or co-lored paper; an expensive process, out of the reach of most self-publishers, since it involves photographing the original full color subject four times, using a different filter to produce a separate negative (called a color separation) for each respective color. The basic four colors are super-imposed in the press operation, which involves running each sheet to be printed through the press four times, making sure that each color *registers* precisely. Some processes involve only 3 colors, others more than 4. For further information, see *Bookmaking*, Appendix 9.

G

GALLEY (galley proofs): originally a metal tray used to store lead type in *letterpress printing*; see *proofs*.

GATHER: placing folded *signatures* in proper order prior to *binding*.

GRAIN: direction of most fibers in a sheet of paper; flow of the wood pulp from which most papers are made creates grain, which should run parallel with the *spine* of a book, to make the book open better and pages lie flat; this fact affects cost of papers and the way in which a sheet may be folded and cut.

GRAPHICS: visual or art *copy* as opposed to text; see *illustrations*.

GUTTER: inner margin of a page; the blank space from the copy to the edge that will be bound; see sketch for *layout*.

H

HALFTONE: see *illustration*.

HAND BINDING: see *binding*.

HAND LETTERING: may tempt you, to reduce book costs, but not recommended; even a practiced commercial artist has difficulty producing lettering as professional and finished-looking as demanded by *offset,* and far from the quality produced by *letterpress* or even *press-type.* The tendency is to try to draw fancy types, which are seldom as readable as commercial ones, even if well-drawn; in addition, only an artist with a great deal of practice in inking can produce a letter with lines that flow smoothly to reproduce well under the fierce eye of a camera, which magnifies any flaws; see also *lettering guides*.

HEAD (headline): title of chapter, section or individual works such as poems; distinguished from running head, the title repeated on consecutive pages of a book. Head also is used to refer to the top of a page, as in *headband*. See *type style*.

HEADBAND: decorative band at top, bottom of the spine of a hardbound book, one way of distinguishing a good quality book from one with inferior *binding;* will

95

be mentioned by the printer in his
bid if it is to be included in costs.

HOT TYPE: molten lead cast into lines of type
for *letterpress* printing; see *cold type*.

I

IBM TYPEWRITER: becoming one of the most accessible, efficient machines for preparing clear, legible, black on white *copy* for *offset printing;* compare the often fuzzy letters produced by an ordinary typewriter to the clean impressions of any carbon ribbon typewriter. A number of companies now offer carbon ribbon typewriters that might be satisfactory for short-term use, but the IBM is the most durable, offers the greatest variety in type styles and models, and because they're so popular you can find many used, rebuilt and rental machines.

IBM manufactures two typewriters and a type composer that can be used by self-publishers. The Selectric II (on which copy for this book is being prepared) features type characters on a rolling ball, easily changeable for type variations. A correcting ribbon is attached so that errors can be lifted from the page--much more cleanly in terms of *camera ready copy* than any form of covering the error and typing over it.

One of the greatest advantages to use of a carbon ribbon machine for setting copy is its availability; whether you rent, buy or borrow, it's right there

in your working area, eliminating your
dependence on the schedule of *typesetters* who have other responsibilities.
If you want to do *pasteup* at 3 a.m. and
find an error in copy, you need not
wait until three days later when the
typesetter can get to it--you can go
directly to your machine and make the
correction yourself. Since time is
frequently defined as money, think of
this factor alone as saving zillions.

Drawbacks to the IBM system: typesetting
machines normally feature "proportional
spacing"; that is, letters are spaced
according to their individual sizes,
whereas the ordinary typewriter and
the Selectric both allot equal space
to every letter in the alphabet. For
most readers, however, this is a bare-
ly noticeable matter. Also, type from
such typewriters often looks better if
slightly reduced; ask your printer a-
bout preparing the pasteup 25% larger
than its final size and reducing the
entire page. And finally, to switch
to italics, you must remove the regular element, insert the italic element,
then switch back; for a book with many
italics, this can be time-consuming.

The IBM Executive is recommended by
some printers because it features proportional spacing; however in other
respects it is an ordinary typewriter
and has only one type face per machine.
I think for one or two books you'd benefit more from a Selectric. Remember

that you might be able to borrow or rent either of these machines; check with your school system and your IBM or other carbon ribbon dealer. If you want to buy one on limited funds, check repair shops; be sure to test the machine thoroughly and remember the only guaranteed machines come from IBM.

The IBM Composer is a dream machine, useful only if you plan to continue producing books or open a print shop. Several models exist, with varying degrees of built in memory for automatic typesetting and corrections, as well as various type faces, proportional spacing and automatic justification devices. However, the cheapest of these is around $9000; if you are still interested, consult your IBM dealer; see *typesetting* for other alternatives.

ILLUSTRATION (graphics, art): in printing, illustrations fall into two broad classes: *line* illustrations and *half-tones*. A line illustration is a drawing composed entirely of solid areas or lines of a single tone; a simple sketch like most of those in this book is an example, as are the printed words on the page; neither contain shadings, only solid black on a white background. Even if it is printed in another solid color, such an illustration is still a line illustration and may be reproduced simply by being photographed; for this reason it may, if the correct size, be placed directly in *pasteup;* line shots are the simplest types of illustrations, and cheapest to reproduce.

Linoleum cuts or block prints, if cut in solid black and white, will print as cleanly as a line shot and can be dramatic illustrations at little cost. Note that all illustrations in this book are line shots to reduce cost.

Fototype supplies a set of screens that can be attached to a Polaroid Land Camera to create pre-screened photos which can be copied without the extra step required by halftones; write Fototype, Inc., 1414 Roscoe St., Chicago IL 60657 for more information.

Halftones contain various shadings or gradations of tones and require more complex forms of *reproduction;* examples are photos, paintings or pencil drawings with shading. If you examine a photo in a newspaper or magazine closely or under a magnifying glass, you will see that what appear to be tones of black or gray are actually thousands of tiny dots which vary in diamater in proportion to the darkness of the tone in that area of the illustration. If you hold the illustration at some distance, the dots seem to blend into an even tone. Reproduction of a halftone is done by photographing it through a ruled screen so as to pro-

duce this optical illusion; such reproduction is also called *continuous
tone*.

A striking graphic may be made by
having the cameraman do a dropout
halftone, sometimes referred to as
posterized halftone, by dropping out
all the shades in a regular photo,
leaving only stark blacks and whites.
An example appears at the Glossary
entry on *design*. This process is also
quite inexpensive.

Another simple method of enhancing
graphics is the use of shading or *benday screens*, available with *press-type*.
By cutting the screen to the desired
size and shape, peeling off the pro-
tective covering and applying the design to the illustration, you can add
shades and patterns to a simple line
shot. Remember that this means it must
be treated as a halftone by the camera
man, a more expensive process.

A black and white photograph may also
be reproduced in two colors for more
depth; the resulting illustration is
called a *duotone*. Less expensive than
full color reproduction, duotones can be
effective but are more costly than simple
black and white halftones. See also *color*
and Appendix 3 for sources of illustration.

IMPRINT: name of publisher, with location
and year of publication, placed at the
bottom of the title page; sometimes
the *logo* is included.

I NDIVIDUAL PRESSES: see *small presses, cooperative publishing, vanity publishers.*

I NTERNATIONAL STANDARD BOOK NUMBER (ISBN): facilitates ordering your book by libraries and booksellers, especially overseas. Each publisher is assigned a prefix number and a set of numbers for each succeeding book. If you plan to publish only one book, it is nonessential. More information may be obtained by writing International Standard Book Numbering Agency, 1180 Avenue of the Americas, NY NY 10036; there is no charge. If you use an IS BN, it should be included with price on the back cover of the book. This book's ISBN is 0-917624-11-4; the initial 7 letters are the prefix of Lame Johnny Press; the latter 3 designate this specific book, whether the title and author are listed or not.

I NTERNATIONAL STANDARD SERIAL NUMBER (ISSN): serves, for magazines, the same purpose as ISBN but is obtained from the Library of Congress, Washington DC 20540.

I NVOICE: bill for goods or services delivered; book distributors will treat you more professionally if your invoices are printed with your company name and address; quick-print will do. Or buy blank pads containing carbons in an office supply store and use a rubber stamp to apply your name and address. Your bookeeping

will be simplified if you type invoices
with a carbon (the second sheet need not
be printed) so that you keep a copy for
your own files. Below is an example of a
simple invoice form. Many orders carry an
order number which must be placed on the
outside of the package; in case you need
to refer later to that order, you should
have it on your invoice copy. The date
helps you trace shipments if they do
not arrive on schedule.

NAME_____

ADDRESS_____.

_____

ORDER NUMBER_____DATE SENT_____

CONSIGNED_____PAID_____DUE_____

QUANTITY_____TITLE_____PRICE____TOTAL____

Lame Johnny Press
Box 66
Hermosa SD 57744
605 255-4228

J

JACKET: see *dust jacket.*

JOB: any printed work while it is in
the printer's hands; "How are you
coming on that Lame Johnny job?"
whether it's a single page news
release or a 384-page book.

JOBBER: a large company which buys at low *discount* to supply books to libraries,
schools and other institutions; the
jobber expects a discount of 20-25%
only, and makes money because it deals
in volume, and in books that sell quickly.

JOB PRINTER: prints brochures, business cards,
forms, stationery and sometimes book
jackets, as opposed to a printer who
specializes in books or magazines;
some job printers now have *quick-
print* capabilities as well.

JUSTIFY: to space out words in a typed line so
lines come out even at both ends; this
is traditional for books, partly because regular typesetting equipment
does the job automatically; becoming
less traditional among small publishers
because of the method involved, as
shown:

Many printers now feel that unjusti-/ |
fied copy, if typed with a fairly//// 4
even right margin, is as attractive// 2
as the old style of justifying by ty- 0

ping the line and counting spaces//// 4
left. When the line is retyped, the// 2
extra spaces are hidden in the line// 2
so that both right and left margins// 2
are even.

Many printers now feel that unjustified copy, if typed with a fairly
even right margin, is as attractive
as the old style of justifying by typing the line and counting spaces
left. When the line is retyped, the
extra spaces are hidden in the line
so that both right and left margins
are even.

Many small publishers feel, as I do,
that it is almost as disturbing to
find extra white space in the middle
of the line as to see an uneven right
margin. The time required for typing
copy with fairly even, but not mathe-
matically counted, right margins is
less than half that required for justification.

L

LADDER DIAGRAM: used to determine pages opposite each other in the completed book; on the top line place the number of the last page of the book and the number of the first page of the book, with a line drawn down the center of the page between them. Then proceed to number as shown, by hand.

20	1
2	19
18	3
4	17
16	5
6	15
14	7
8	13
12	9
10	11

When doing *pasteup*, use a double page arrangement, making a *layout* large enough to do two pages at once. For example, you will be working on page 16

at the same time that you are working
on page 5.

A trick for being sure you have ar-
anged pages correctly is to remember
that the total of the two opposing pages
is always one more than the total of
pages in your book; thus if you are
doing a 20-page book, pages 12 and 9
appear in the ladder diagram opposite
one another, because they total 21.

L AYOUT: refined from original plan (*dummy*),
describes the working diagram of a
single typical page or an entire book,
as well as the process of producing
that diagram. The position of each item
is shown in detail, including margins,
spacing of text, placement of graphics,
page numbers; there must be a fixed place
for each element of the *page design*;
pasteup follows layout.

To prepare a layout, tape a large
sheet of paper to the *light table*.
Outline on it the dimensions of the
finished book, for example 5½ x(by)
8½. Inside these lines, draw the actual margins of the page, keeping in
mind that *trim size* is as much as
3/8" smaller than finished size. The
margin should be ½" as an absolute
minimum; 3/4 to 1 inch is better. I
prefer to work in two-page spreads
as shown and as discussed in *ladder
diagram*.

Once you have determined the pattern
for a single page, all subsequent
pages must follow it; therefore your

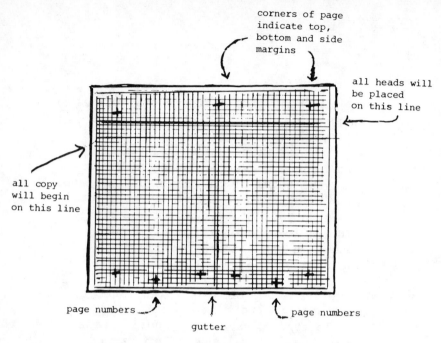

corners of page indicate top, bottom and side margins

all heads will be placed on this line

all copy will begin on this line

page numbers

gutter

page numbers

plan must include a place for all elements that will appear anywhere in the book, so that each item appears in balance, planned for, and all pages are uniform. This is not mere convention but helps establish a professional appearance for your book. For example, if the first three chapters have single line titles, but the fourth has a subtitle, space for that subtitle must be included in the layout for the first three chapters. Or if you've decided to place one poem per page, and have some with short lines and some with long, select a left margin that will allow both to look balanced on the page.

If copy is to be set in two columns, this would be indicated by vertical lines at appropriate places on the layout.

Or you might indicate the placement of poems and headlines in this manner:

The poem
would
move down
the page
in this
manner,
with allow-
ance made
for variations
in line length

heads, authors' names

Remember to indicate placement of all
types of *headlines* and plan handling
of all *graphics*. Page numbers may appear at center top or bottom, or you
might prefer to place odd numbers at
upper or lower right and even numbers
at upper or lower left (odd pages are
always right hand pages, even always
left hand). Once you've established
the layout pattern, you simply place
blank sheets over it for each new page
in *pasteup*.

After layout is completed, ask your printer which method of pasteup he prefers.
Even though you do layout in two-page
spreads, you may still want to do *pasteup*
on single pages. If you do, keep checking
to be sure copy on pages actually opposite
one another in the finished book will
balance aesthetically, and read correctly.

LAYOUT PAPER (cross section paper): sometimes
used interchangeably to refer to paper with a grid of light blue (nonreproducing)lines; sizes vary; sometimes supplied by printers. Since

light blue is not picked up by the
camera, layouts may be done directly
on this paper, or it may be used in
drawing your own layout to be taped
to the surface of the light table.

This drawing shows how graph paper is
divided into squares; beside it I'll tape
an actual piece of graph paper to demon-
strate its invisibility to the camera.

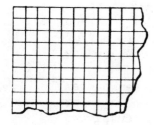

While the paper is very convenient,
it's also expensive and really not
necessary. Instead, prepare a layout as described above and use plain
white paper for individual pages; I
like 16 lb. bond as I can see through
it, yet it's durable enough to stand
handling; see also *pasteup*.

LEAF: two pages; see *page*.

LEGEND: explanation of an *illustration*;
usually refers to maps; see *caption*.

LETTERING GUIDES (stencils, templates): may
seem to be good substitutes for *press-*

type or *hand lettering*; however, letters designed to be inked are not very readable--compare them to other *type styles*. Even with a rapidograph pen, which does the best job of inking on such stencils, a great deal of practice is needed to keep letters even in shading and to prevent ink from flowing out under the edges of the stencil, creating a blot. Not recommended. *Templates* in shapes--graduated circles, squares, ovals and curves--are often useful for shaping illustrations or photos; see *crop*.

LETTERPRESS PRINTING: oldest, most versatile of modern printing methods, in which printing is done directly from the raised type; type is cast from molten metal and the inked image is transferred directly to the paper; produces a crisp, image, with an actual impression in the surface of the paper; an experienced printer can tell the difference between a book printed by *offset* and one printed letterpress by running his calloused, inky finger over the surface of the page. Letterpress is now often more expensive than offset because the equipment, and people skilled in its use, is not readily available. Some small press publishers are learning to hand set type and print on small letterpress systems for the sheer beauty of the product, but that is an entire subject in itself; such printers may be located by reference to *The International Directory of Little Magazines and Small Presses*.

For a more complete definition of letterpress printing, see *Pocket Pal,* Appendix 9.

LETTERSPACING: amount of space between letters in a *type face;* generally refers to the space between letters in *heads;* see *press-type.*

LIBRARY OF CONGRESS CATALOG CARD NUMBER: a card catalog, with numbers preassigned to forthcoming books, is maintained in the Library's Card Division; subscribers to the library's catalog card service are thus able to order cards by number and thus eliminate a search fee; this is a service which facilitates order of your book by libraries, boosting sales. The number should be requested at least 3 months before publication of the book. Write for information to the CIP (Cataloging in Publication) Office, Library of Congress, Washington DC 20540, listing the following information:
1. full name of author or editor
2. title of the book
3. whether or not this is a new edition
4. date of publication (approximate)
5. name and address of publisher and/or printer
6. series title and number, if the book is part of a series
7. whether or not the book is part of a serial publication
8. whether or not the book will be copyrighted

112

9. approximate number of pages (books under 50 pages are not given L of C numbers
10. type of binding

Not all books are accepted for the Card Division; there is no charge for this service, though you should send a copy of the book to the CIP Office as soon as it is printed.

L IGHT TABLE: opaque glass, mounted horizontally with a light source under it for *layout* and *pasteup*. Placing a layout on the light table, you may put clean sheets of paper over it and proceed to align material correctly along the lines of the original plan without having to re-draw them on each page, since the light passes through several layers of paper. Thus you can achieve accuracy in pasteup without marking the finished page more than necessary; a light table is the single most important tool in self-publishing. The accompanying sketches show two possible styles: the light table, where it is customary to work standing up, and the light board, which may be placed on a table or desk. Commercial models of both are available but cost $150 and up, whereas my light table was built for under $30, including labor. Essentials in a light table include:

1. glass surface so that cutting copy does not harm the working area;
2. a light source under the work surface; fluorescent lights minimize glare;

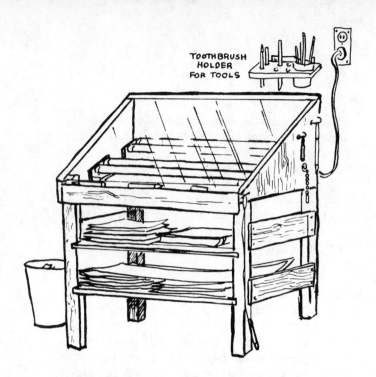

TOOTHBRUSH
HOLDER
FOR TOOLS

3. an opaque glass surface to minimize
eyestrain; this can be done by spray-
ing a fine coat of white paint or taping a single layer of tracing paper
to the reverse side of the glass;
4. back strain is lessened if the surface is the correct height and tilted
slightly downward;
5. a ledge at the front of the work
surface catches pens, *x-acto blades*
and other items that would normally
roll off; you might not really appre-
ciate this feature until you have an
x-acto blade stuck in the top of your
toe.
6. Convenient but nonessential additions to the table include: a button
on the cord to turn off the light,
rather than unplugging it; a wall behind the table for hanging tools; a
gadget like that to the right of the
light table (actually a toothbrush

holder) for tape, knives and other
small items; a shelf or two under the
work surface for pasteup paper, *acetate, press-type,* layout sheets. At
least one authority says you can do
layout against a window; unless you
have a one-page job or are super-
human and not subject to shoulder
strain, don't try it. See *Printing
It,* Appendix 9, for more on work surfaces.

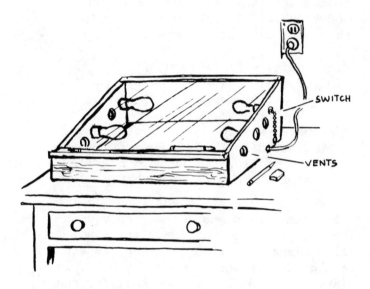

LIMITED EDITION: most self-published work
    could be designated "limited" since total
    number of books printed seldom exceeds

10,000; such a designation increases the book's immediate value as well as its ultimate attractiveness to collectors. Books may also be signed by author and/or numbered to increase their value. Many small publishers price a signed and/or numbered edition several dollars above the regular edition. A limited edition should be designated by printing, either early in the book (perhaps in acknowledgements or on the copyright page) or with the *colophon,* this or a similar statement:

"This edition of ___(title)___ is limited to 1000 (or the number you intend to print) copies."

A numbered edition, on the other hand, is indicated in this manner: "This edition of _(title)_ is limited to 1000 copies of which this is number_____."

When typing the statement, include the title and the number of copies you intend to prepare, but leave the final line blank. After publication, insert the number in these copies by hand, in ink. For an author-signed edition, the statement might read: "This edition of __(title)_ is limited to (number) copies, of which _(number)_ are signed by the author." The author then signs each copy individually below the statement. Do not use a stamp for the author's name, as this makes the signature valueless to the collector.

Remember each separate edition must have

a separate ISBN number; that is, if you publish a regular edition, a signed edition and a numbered edition, you must assign three different ISBN numbers and three prices. And don't underrate your book's appeal to collectors; many specialize in odd ways, wanting only signed copies printed in Abilene, for example, or books of poetry of any kind so long as they are signed by the author.

LINE COPY: may be reproduced without using a *halftone* screen; such copy may be pasted up directly and photographed along with type elements, eliminating the extra processes required for halftone reproduction and thus reducing costs; also called a line shot; see *illustration*.

LINE GAGE: see *pica*.

LINE SPACING: amount of space between lines, known as leading (since it originated with *letterpress printing* where pieces of lead were placed between lines); this spacing is always expressed in *points*; there is no set rule for the amount of space, but printers can recommend spacing depending on what looks best with each kind of type; you may request any amount of space between lines or letters, simply by writing instructions for the *typesetter* in the margin. See *Bookmaking*, Appendix 9.

LIST PRICE: see *cover price*.

LOGO: name and/or special design used by company or product as a trademark or in advertising; appears on all its products. At left, the logo of Lame Johnny Press, a fanciful drawing representing Lame Johnny reading a book.

Some of my other favorites include the logos of Toothpaste Press (one of the finest letterpress printers in the na-

tion); Pentagram Press (another); Juniper Press (still another); and Territorial Press. All are located in the upper midwest; find their addresses in the *International Directory,* Appendix 9.

LOWER CASE: small letters, distinguished from capital letters; abbreviated "lc"; when referring to the usual combination of capitals and lower case letters, the abbreviation is clc or c & lc; distinguished from caps and small capitals, c & sc.

M: printer's standard abbreviation for 1,000;
in "Number of copies: 5M"; always
capitalized.

MAILING: if you plan to mail only one book, go
directly to your nearest post office
and get the most recent *Mailers Guide,*
which covers such important matters as
what you can send under the differing
classes of mail, special mailing services, proper addressing and zip codes.
Important excerpts appear below.

"Third class mail consists of circu-
lars, booklets, catalogs and other
printed materials such as newsletters,
corrected proof sheets with manuscript
copy, not otherwise required as first
class mail. . . . Each piece of third
class mail is limited in weight to
less than 16 ounces. The same material
weighing 16 ounces or more is classified as fourth class, or parcel post,
mail. There are two categories of third
class mail: single piece and bulk." The
latter requires that you pay a yearly
fee, mail all pieces at once at a single post office, and mail at least 200
identical pieces. If you plan to do
more than one book, you might investi-
gate bulk rates further for sending
promotional material.

"The special fourth class rate applies,

in general, to books of 24 pages or more of which at least 22 are printed, ... Each parcel is endorsed 'Special 4th Class Rate' plus a description of the item, such as 'Books'. . . . (Categories of material not qualifying for this rate include books containing advertising for other merchandise. . . .

"There are two different and distinct provisions for mailing specific materials at the library rate of postage. The following materials qualify for the library rate when they are loaned or exchanged between schools, colleges, libraries or certain non-profit organizations and libraries and their readers: books, periodicals, bound theses. . . . The following materials qualify for the library rate when they are mailed by or to, schools, colleges, libraries or certain non-profit organizations: 16 millimeter or narrower width films, sound recordings, certain museum materials . . . . Interested customers should consult their local Postmaster or Customer Service Representative for detailed information on the conditions which apply to mailings under the library rate."

I haven't mentioned specific postal rates, because no doubt they will have risen voluminously by the time you read this. Before mailing large quantities of books, compare Postal Service rates with rates and delivery re-

cords and schedules of other mail car-
riers in your area, such as United
Parcel Service. UPS is generally cheaper
and more efficient, especially for large
orders. Most small publishers now use the
Postal Service only for single copies and
send everything else through UPS.

Packaging is another important aspect
of mailing, especially given Postal
Service inefficiency in delivering
third and fourth class mail. In order
to insure that your books get to your
customers undamaged--which is really
part of your job--you'll need: filament wrapping tape; gummed address
labels; a rubber stamp that reads
"Special 4th Class Book Rate" and
perhaps another with your return address; padded mailing envelopes; a
heavy duty stapler; invoice forms
which you can type and have quick-
printed or purchase, with carbons.

All of these items can be obtained at
wholesale prices from a paper company
if you have given yourself a company
name; the savings is worth it (13¢ for
an 11 x 14 mailing envelope as compared
to 50¢ at an office supply store) and
you may not have to pay sales tax. A
good work area should be established,
with mailing tools close to books, and
a wrapping surface. I suggest you keep
a mailing list of everyone who orders
a book, filed in zip code order and/or
typed on stickon address labels--which
can often be xeroxed directly onto self-
adhesive labels the next time you need

to mail a promotional piece to the entire list.

Be professional about making out invoices and including them with orders. I find it easier to fill orders correctly if I type all labels at once, indicating in my own code right on the label what the customer has ordered and whether or not he's paid for it; also type order numbers on the label for the customer's benefit. Then I go through orders again, typing all required invoices, filling out the forms required by libraries and schools. At this point I make sure the person or institution is included in my mailing list. Then I proceed to the mailing area with labels and invoices, and recheck each order as I wrap books.

Don't try to substitute masking tape for filament tape; postal regulations suggest the stronger type for the excellent reason that it's needed to withstand the sorting machines (referred to in the publishing business as "crushers") in larger cities. Almost every piece of fourth class mail that goes more than 100 miles has to survive a sorter, so protect it with the same care with which you published it. Padded envelopes might be bypassed for several layers of grocery bags, if you're only mailing a few books. Or wrap each book in a sheet of newsprint or other waste paper, before

placing it in the mailing envelope; this
will help protect it and add little to
the cost.

M AILING LISTS: names and addresses of people who
may have reason to buy your book, as
opposed to a simple random list. A number of agencies sell or rent lists
classified in various ways: all the
people who have bought earthworms; all
professors of English, or all those who
teach seminars in the poetry of Robert
Lowell; every one who has bought an
electric toothbrush. If you are publishing a book on repair methods for electric toothbrushes, your list selects
itself. If your book is on a subject
less specifically limited, you must
decide if people who buy earthworms
would buy your book of earthworm re-
cipes. See app. 7 for sources of readymade lists. When ordering, always ask
about use: many companies rent lists
for one-time use only.

In conjunction with, or instead of,
buying or renting lists, you can develop your own. I tear the address
from the envelope or order and stuff
it in a file. When I'm snowed in for
three days or some similar calamity
befalls, I type addresses on sheets
of gummed labels (available in office
supply stores). The labels I use come
33 to a sheet; I leave the 3 across
the top blank so I can describe the
names on that sheet. You might also
want to group addresses alphabetically
or by zip code to facilitate elimina-
tion of duplicate names. **123**

These labels can then be xeroxed directly onto other labels--so you keep the master list and use it only when needed. The xerox machine I use (in an office supply store, at 10¢/sheet) cuts off the top 3 labels--another reason for leaving them blank. To update lists, get a rubber stamp (or printed envelopes) reading "Address Correction Requested" and stamp in the upper left corner by your return address on bulk mailings; they'll be returned at a small fee with the new address if the Postal Service has it, or marked "Addressee Unknown" so you can delete that name from your list. Over a few years, if you're publishing material with a particular slant or style, your own mailing list will constantly improve. And once someone from a rented list orders from you, transfer the name to your list. You might include return envelopes or order blanks with mailings; I think this increases orders from individuals. Or you might develop an order blank on a postage-paid postcard, which contains ordering information and exerpts from a review of the book. Check with the Postal Service; envelopes or postcards must be printed with a specific return form, but you pay only for those actually returned, and the fee is slightly higher than that for first-class mail. If you've established a regular clientele, it's worth the expense, which can be built into the price of the book.

If you are so inclined, a number of other agencies, including some of those listed in Appendix 7, will pay as much as 10¢ per name for your mailing list. You could make a little extra money by selling your list selectively to companies with similar interests--but consider whether you want to subject your customers to added mailings over which you have no control.

MAIL ORDER: often, sales will be direct to a real live customer responding to a reading or other public appearance, and the transaction will be in cash. Simple accounting methods should enable you to keep track of these sales effectively. But what about mail order? As soon as the book is offered for sale, you will get inquiries from libraries, bookstores and others using a whole new set of confusing terms, asking about your *discount* rate, requiring invoices in triplicate, asking if you allow *returns* for credit.

The simplest way to deal with this is to sell only at the *cover price,* with no discount. However, you'll lose some sales this way, since many distributors rely on discounts. If you plan to sell a major portion of your books through bookstores and other distributors, set the *cover price* high enough to allow for these discounts and to allow at least one dollar for mailing costs; see *discount*.

Never send an order, even for one
book, C.O.D. or with an invoice,
unless you feel you can afford to
lose the money. Institutions can in
general be trusted, but with individual orders require that payment
accompany or precede fulfillment of
the order.

Mailing is time-consuming but can be
made less so by organization and a
selection of supplies; see *mailing*.
If you are working in a school, perhaps sales of the book could be taken over by an accounting class as
a project.

Terms used by customers are varied;
many are self-explanatory. If you
need additional help, turn to *The
Bookman's Glossary*, Appendix 9.

MAKE-READY: all operations to prepare *job*
for the press once it reaches printer;
in *letterpress* it means specifically
leveling of forms as they are placed
on the press.

MAKEUP: assembling varied elements of *pasteup*
into finished pages, and the pages
into a finished form for printing.

MANUSCRIPT PREPARATION: some standards help
maintain accuracy, even if you are
typesetting copy that you have written. Double space, on one side of
sturdy white paper; remember a manuscript takes a lot of abuse in the
course of typesetting and being used

126

for *proofreading*. Use standard 8½ by 11 paper, a black ribbon and a typewriter with clean standard (not elite and definitely not script) type. Indent all paragraphs, though you may not want them indented on copy. Allow about an inch margin all around the manuscript for the printer's instructions to typesetters.

Type your name and/or the book's title at the top of each page, with the number of the page, and number each page consecutively straight through the manuscript, placing "end" on the last sheet. (Do not number by chapters because if a printer drops the manuscript, it will be more difficult to get in order). Do not staple pages to together as typesetting requires they be laid aside as they are typed. Be consistent; try to type the same number of lines per page to help in estimating the total length of the manuscript. Start new chapters about 1/3 down from the top of the page, and indicate chapter number and complete chapter title. Check all names, dates, facts carefully; double check spellings, have someone who is unfamiliar with the manuscript, but literate, go over it for errors. Treat the manuscript as you would treat any important college research paper.

Always use a carbon so that you have a record of the manuscript; make corrections first in ink, not pencil, on the carbon, then transcribe them to the original. The manuscript need not be typed perfectly as long as corrections are legible. Use standard *copyreader's marks* for clarity if your book is going to a typesetter. Corrections should never be made on the back of the sheet, in the left margin, or on attached slips which are easily lost. When the manuscript is completed, keep the corrected carbon and send the more readable original to the printer. The more nearly perfect the manuscript, the less cost to you in time or money.

MECHANICAL: another term for *camera ready copy* or *pasteup* of all elements on one page, before the plate has been made in *offset printing*.

MIMEOGRAPH: works by forcing ink through stencil onto a piece of paper; the history of printing and revolution would be much different without the mimeograph, that cheap and handy printing machine for anyone with an axe to grind; with a typewriter and a mimeograph--or even a pencil and a mimeograph--you can be in print very quickly. However quality cannot be compared to that of any decent printing system, and since the public identifies quality of print with quality of content, I don't recommend a mimeographed publication if you plan to sell or otherwise distribute your work. An electronic stencil cutter which can scan a finished *pasteup* and transfer it to a stencil for mimeograph printing exists, but even this expensive advance (the device costs

128

about $1500 new) doesn't produce very
good images. If, however, you need to
produce ephemeral material--news releases, handouts, broadsheets and
other one-sheet publications not intended to last--investigate A.B. Dick
or Gestetner mimeograph systems. See
also *quick-print; Printing It,* App. 9.

MULTICOLOR: achieving variety by application of one ink color to white or
tinted stock; occasionally two applied
ink colors can be used to create an
effect of color less expensively than
four-color process, but more cheaply,
by careful attention to the blend between the ink and tint of the stock.
Consult your printer for his capabilities and suggestions. See *black
and white*.

NEWSPRINT: paper made of ground wood pulp and small amounts of chemical pulp; used for printing newspapers; not durable and should not be used for any printing job that is expected to last since it yellows and disintegrates; see *paper*.

NRB PENCIL: nonreproducing blue pencil, to *crop marks*, *layout* marks and some *proofreading*; can be used lightly on *camera ready offset copy* because it does not show up in photographic plate; in some cases, any light blue pencil will do; check with your printer.

NUMBER OF PAGES: even experienced printers have trouble estimating pages sometimes, but you can show your manuscript to a printer and ask his opinion and get something close to accuracy.

For prose, first count the number of words in 10 typical full lines on a number of typical pages and divide by 10. This will give you the average number of words per line. Then count the number of lines on a typical full page, counting all the lines, no matter how few words they contain. Third, count the number of pages in the entire manuscript and multiply the number of words per line by the number of lines per page. Then multiply the resulting figure by the number of pages. This gives you the number of words in the text of your manuscript with some accuracy. The problem now is to estimate, depending on what type you are using and on line spacing, how many of those words will fit on each printed page. For an average figure, based on the kind of type and spacing used in most books, divide the total number of words in the text by 350. This will give you an educated guess on the number of printed pages in the text. If your book is divided into chapters, add ½ page for each chapter; also add all the preliminary and back pages. Most printers work in multiples of 16 pages (a *signature*) so for purposes of estimating you should assume that your book will print out to the next higher number of pages divisible by 16. (Multiples of 16 are 32, 48, 64, 80, 96, 112). If you come out with an estimate of 90 pages, use 96 pages for obtaining *bids*.

If your manuscript is poetry, allow a maximum of 37 lines per page, remembering that spaces between stanzas count as one line, as does the title and the space before it. If there are especially long lines that may have to be broken by the printer, allow two lines for them. Stylistically, poetry looks best if each poem begins on a new page; remember to add the preliminary and back pages and bring the book up to a multiple of 16.

OFFSET LITHOGRAPHY: fastest growing and newest of modern print methods; the most important thing for the small publisher to know is that an offset press can print, economically, in black and white, anything that can be photographed. Therefore, if you want to type a manuscript clearly with a new ribbon on sturdy white paper, your book can be printed directly from those sheets, without further *typesetting*. *Illustrations* that fit the pages can also be printed, as can collages, pencil sketches--anything in tones of black and white.

Technically, lithographic offset involves transferring ink twice between printing plate and the sheet of paper being printed. The image is first transferred from the plate to a rubberized blanket and from this it is "offset" onto the paper; the process is chemically based on the principle that oil and water do not mix. This method creates a clearer impression on a wider variety of paper surfaces than is possible in *letterpress*, with less adjustment. For a more complete, and more technical, explanation, see *Pocket Pal,* Appendix 9.

OPACITY: ability of printing paper to prevent matter on the opposite side from showing through; show-through reduces legibility and cheapens the publication. Printers often discuss the show-through quality of paper.

OPAQUE: to paint out negative areas not wanted on the *plate*; differs from *opacity* of paper.

ORIGINAL: may refer to *copy* after it has been *typeset* to differentiate this from *proof* copies; may also refer to the actual *pasteup* as opposed to proof copies.

OVERLAY: see *color*.

OVERRUN: copies printed in addition to those ordered. Since mistakes, machinery breakdown or other factors make it virtually impossible for a printer to be sure of printing precisely the number of publications ordered, most contracts provide for a 5 to 10 per cent over- or underrun. You may also ask for a price on overrun copies of the book, which would be printed later from the same plates, at a lower price than the original since camera work is already completed. In addition, you may order overrun dust jackets for promotional purposes; see *promotion*.

P

PAGE: one side of a *leaf* or *sheet;* each leaf or sheet contains two pages, front and back.

PAGE ARRANGEMENT: the three portions of a book preliminary pages (or front matter), text, and back pages (or back matter). Not every book needs every page listed below; select those that are essential for your purpose. Each sheet or leaf of paper contains two pages--the front and the back; all right hand pages will be odd numbered and all left hand pages even numbered.

Preliminary pages include the following:

end papers: a four-page section of plain or decoratively printed paper necessary in quality hardbound books to hold the inside front and back covers to the first and last pages of the book;

bastard title or half title: the first printed page of a book, consisting of the main title only; often eliminated in softbound books; the page following it, the back of the half title, is usually blank;

title page: lists the full title of the book, any subtitle, name of author or editor, statement about any re-

visions or previous editions and the
name of the publisher;

copyright page: may not be eliminated
if you want the rights to your book
protected; see *copyright* for information to be placed on this page, which
should also contain the *Library of
Congress number* and *International
Standard Book Number;* to facilitate
orders, you should place your mailing
address and the book's price here, and
if you wish to credit the printer, this
is one place, though you may prefer to
list him in the *colophon;*

dedication: not essential; the back of
this page is left blank;

epigraph: not essential; usually consists of a pertinent quotation that
sets the tone of your book; if included, it should be on a right hand
page;

contents: also a right-hand page and
should not be run over onto the back
of that page; if a longer contents is
needed, you might begin on a left hand
page and design the two facing pages
to complement each other; should include title, chapter number and beginning page number of each section of
the book; actual page numbers must
be inserted after the *pasteup* has been
made and you are certain which elements
appear on each page;

list of illustrations, list of tables:

if your book has a number of illustrations, tables, graphs or other such information, it is a convenience for the reader to list such material for ready reference in the front of the book;

foreword: a statement about the book by someone other than the author; should begin on a right hand page and list the name of the writer and his title at the end; not essential;

preface: a statement by the author about the book, his reasons for writing it, methods of research; should be relatively short, begin on a right hand page and need not be signed;

acknowledgements: if few, may be added to the preface; if they are extensive they should be separate and begin on a right hand page; should include permissions granted for previously printed work and any appropriate thanks; not essential;

Text pages are the body of the book; their arrangement is discussed in *page design*; chapter headings may be on separate pages, or you may simply want to drop the top margin down several inches before placing the chapter title; poetry is generally arranged with each poem on a new page;

Back pages:

appendices: supplementary information that would disturb the flow of the book, or that is simply easier for the reader to find in this location;

notes on the text are often placed at the back of the book to facilitate reading the text; often these are in smaller types;

glossary: unfamiliar terms are often included at the back of the book for reader convenience;

bibliography: listed so the reader may do additional research;

index: information in a technical book should be made more accessible by listing words of importance, names, places, subjects in alphabetical order with the pages on which they appear;

colophon: a holdover from the days when books were fine art objects, but you may want to revive it to give your book additional class.

PAGE DESIGN: arrangement of elements needed on a page for the most attractive and readable book; these include text, *headlines, graphics,* page numbers. Special pages, such as contents, which are often just dull lists, should be given extra consideration. Title and copyright pages and chapter openings are other pages that might be enlivened by imaginative placement of type.

In designing a page, consider first
the margins; will the book have a single line of copy extending from side
margin to side margin, or will it be
divided into columns? Equal width columns or unequal? (Note that the unequal columns in this book have been
made part of the book's total design by
furnishing white space to enliven pages
on which no illustrations appear, and
into which illustrations and other
information may extend to gain attention.)

You might want to assemble the elements of your pages and try a variety of placements, as I have done
in some of the examples following.
See *Bookmaking* for some good examples,
especially of handling front matter.

One possible arrangement of the contents
page of this book; compare with those following and with the arrangement and type
face selected.

Contents

138

Contents

Contents

Contents

Contents page from *A Country for Old Men
And Other Stories*, a collection of short
fiction by E.R. Zietlow, published by
Lame Johnny Press.

thumb prints

by

st. joseph school students

cover by cindy thies

state publishing co.
pierre, south dakota
1976

The title page of *thumb prints*, published in 1976 by grade school students and teachers at St. Joseph's School in Pierre, South Dakota, carries out the design theme of having each child hand print his/her own page--though this printing was done by an adult.

NOT COMING TO BE BARKED AT

Poems by Ted Kooser

Pentagram Press Milwaukee, Wisconsin

An attractive, balanced title page from
Pentagram Press.

contents

A simple but beautifully balanced contents page from *The Earth is Tingling at
my Feet,* an anthology of student work
from the Montana Arts Council.

143

A List of the Magical Properties
of a Northern Night

two feathers of a male peacock
the large hand of a clock at rest
several grains of white sugar
a small drop of sweet liqueur
a breath of wind from Canada
the North Star
an eagle's claw
the beak of a dove
a shallow whisper
a young girl dreaming of love

A well-designed page of poetry from Truck
Press, using a suggestion of border to
differentiate between sections of the
book written by different authors.

BUFFALO HEARTS

By Sun Bear

A NATIVE AMERICAN'S VIEW OF INDIAN CULTURE,

RELIGION AND HISTORY

Photographs by courtesy of the Smithsonian Institution,

Washington, D. C.

Copyright 1970, by Sun Bear

SBN Number 911010-86-6 Cloth Edition
SBN Number 911010-87-4 Paper Edition

Naturegraph Publishers, Healdsburg, California 95448

This page loses effectiveness by crowd-
ing: elements from the title page and
copyright have been combined.

Joan Colby

Collector

Thumb and forefinger vised
on an inch of space
poised to pinch
the motionless onionskin wings
perfect as a prayer
offered for no gain.

A fragile epistle
on a green leaf
which his tiptoe
cannot translate.

The impostor eye-mark
looks inward
unsurprised.

The wings rise
crucified gently
on blue air
and his fingers snap
closed the twin pages
on a rare signature.

15

This page looks fragmented because of
the great contrast in size between the
text and heads; use of two different
headline types is disturbing since one
is a display face.

BOOKS

Mother Rabbit's Son. *By Dick Gackenbach.* Harper and Row, 10 East 53rd St., NYC 10022. (4.95)

Two easy-to-read stories about Young Tom, a rabbit who always gets into lots of trouble. He is stubborn and never gives up easily. In one story, Tom eats only Hamburgers, until he learns about better things to eat. In the other story he surprises everyone when he brings home a gigantic creature as his very own household pet. (Ages 4+)

The Golden Age of Comic Books, *By Richard O'Brien* Ballantine, 201 East 50th St. NYC 10022. (6.95)

Goshes! What a fantastic book! It's got 48 classic full color covers of such superheroes as Superman, Batman, Captain Marvel, Green Lantern, Bulletman, and a whole lot more! The main thing wrong is that these proud 'pulp' mag covers are here reproduced on slick inlaid-paper and hi-gloss enamel. It's like silverized baby shoes!

The Way To Play. *By the Diagram Group.* Bantam Books, 666 Fifth Avenue, NYC 10019 320 pp., illus., (7.95)

A well done collection of games, clearly illustrated and explained. Including board games from *snakes and ladders* to *backgammon;* card games from *whist* to *solitaire;* foreign games; ancient games; target games; table games. A total of over 2,000 games and 5,000 color illustrations. Fantastic!!!

The Whole Kids Catalog. *By Peter Cardoza & Ted Menten.* Bantam Books, 666 Fifth Ave., NYC 10019 224 pages, illus., (5.95)

Zeroed into the five to fifteen crowd, this catalog sourcebook has 39 thrilling chapters of alternative activities to television rotting. That's right. If you know of children suffering from "got nothin-ta-doo" stagnation, here is a quick and easily accessible cure. The *Catalog* is loaded with all kinds of things to find, do, make and explore. It may be the last refuge for the unimaginative, but it *really works!* Chapter headings include: art, music, history, indoor/outdoor games, magic tricks, nature, theatre, yoga, cooking, gardening, and carpentry. Already in its 7th printing, this book is necessary for any child's mental survival!

This is an example of an attempt to cram too much information on one page--the page number is almost cut off, and the page is too busy to be readable.

PAPER (stock): usually made of wood pulp; finer grade writing papers are cotton fiber; variations are endless, but you'll need to know about three basic categories: bond paper, book and text papers and cover stock.

Bonds are usually writing papers, made in standard 8½ x 11 or 8½ x 14 sheets; quality varies from flimsy cheap types up to fine sheets made of 100% cotton. The finishes range from very smooth to extra smooth, in colors from pastels to dark, earthy shades. Weights go from 16 lb. (which I use for *pasteup*) to 20 lb. (which I like for typing *copy* because it's sturdy enough to take a lot of handling) and 24 lb. (Weights are based on actual weight of 500 sheets of paper in its full size.)

Book papers are used for many brochures, some magazines and most books; weights vary from 50 lb. to 100 lb, with 60 lb (expressed as 60#) being most commonly used; it is comparable to a 20# bond. Text papers, available in a bewildering array of colors, finishes and edges, are touted by printers and paper salesmen because they are expensive and customers fall in love with textures, colors and finishes easily. But before you get too carried away, consider relative costs. If you can buy a ream of good 20# bond for $3, you'll find that a comparable 60# book costs at least a third again as much, an inexpensive

text double the bond, and a more costly
text three times the bond. Depending
on the job to be printed, the bond
might be quite satisfactory.

Since the weights of the two types of paper are computed differently, it's difficult to explain how to compare them.
You'll simply have to ask your printer to
show you samples of each, and compare by
feel. Also ask his advice on whether
the cheaper paper will do the kind of
job you want it to do, and ask for samples of similar work on that paper. In
my experience printers tend not to care
so much about *opacity* as poets.

In choosing paper for the text of
your book, the primary consideration
is its *opacity*; the stock must be
heavy enough so that printing on one
side does not show through the other
side. The paper should also be of a
color that will allow good readability; avoid dark inks on dark papers,
or contrasts that "hurt the eyes"
if you want the book to be read.
Surfaces must be smooth enough so
printing will be uniform. Again, ask
your printer. Budget and availability
of paper tend to compress your choices;
rely on *design* to give your book the
individuality it demands, rather than
putting money into fancy papers
and colored inks.

Cover papers are anything from a *self
cover* (the same weight as the text pa-

per) through 80# book to 100# book up to cardboard thicknesses. Again, there are varieties of colors, textures, costs, but I recommend selecting something in the 80 to 100# range, in a texture that will enhance your cover design. Some surfaces are so heavily textured that ink won't print uniformly; some papers are so thick they don't fold straight.

In paper selection, as in so many other areas, choose a book with the feel of paper that appeals to you and ask your printer to suggest a comparable quality of stock.

No matter how low your budget, avoid *newsprint* for books. Recycled paper may appeal to you emotionally, but be aware that its quality is sometimes difficult to control--colors vary, and sometimes large chunks of anonymous objects appear in sheets. It's still more expensive than bonds in most cases, though sometimes cheaper than good book paper. Explore it if you're interested, but with care. It's too bad we can't use more of it, because I suspect paper mills try to keep it high because they don't want to have to build in recycling processes; catch-22.

If you become sufficiently immersed in the art of book production to want fine *letterpress printing* on fine paper, consider going one step further and buying handmade paper, or even learning still another profession and making your own. See Appendix 3 for paper makers.

Other terms you'll encounter in discussing paper included: coated, sized, laid and wove; all these refer to type of finish within one or more of the categories mentioned above; ask your printer.

Coated refers to paper surfaced with white clay or a similar substance to provide a smooth printing surface; enamel paper is glossy; dull-coated papers also exist and are more readable since they reflect less light.

Laid is paper which, when held up to the light, shows fine parallel and cross lines; these are produced by the wires of the mold in handmade papers but can be imitated by the pattern on the first roller in a paper-making machine. Wove paper shows no such pattern.

The surface of sized paper has been treated to make it less receptive to water. Blotters are unsized; writing paper is hardsized; offset papers are specially sized to resist the considerable moisture used in the process.

PAPER SIZES: while bond usually comes in 8½ x 11 or 8½ x 14, text and cover stocks are cut from large "mill sheets"--23 x 29,

23 x 35, 25 x 38 or 26 x 40. Since paper must be cut "with the grain" it's easy to waste it by designing an odd size book. Ask your printer to help you choose a size that will produce the least waste, since you pay for all the paper purchased for your job, whether it's in your book or on the floor. If there is to be some trim waste, ask the printer to save it for you; you may never have to buy another piece of stationery! If you live in a large city or do more than one book, you may find large paper warehouses that will let you browse, and pay low prices for fine papers that are left over from bigger jobs. However, in most cases you'll be relying on what your printer has on hand or can readily get. For more on paper sizes, see *Printing It* and *The Shoestring Publisher's Guide*.

PARTS OF BOOK: see *page arrangement*.

PASTEUP: the process of affixing all elements *headlines, copy, illustrations*, page numbers) to individual pages exactly as they will appear in the finished book.

Before pasteup begins, all copy should be trimmed of excess white paper. This is best done on the light table with a triangle and an X-acto knife, as shown. Trimming first will save time and may save you from ruining copy by cutting in haste. Trim with the copy

152

on the inside of the cutting edge, so
that if the knife slips it will slash
harmlessly into white space, not into
typeset copy. If the edge of the copy
tears, change the dull blade at once.
Remember that X-acto knives work because they are sharp, and they can cut
fingers as well as paper. Save any lines

you trim from copy, even the typesetter's comments to himself and lines
with errors; you may need a correction
you haven't provided for later--even
a single letter--and you can nip it

out of an extra line instead of re-
setting the incorrect word.

The next step in pasteup is to tape
the prepared *layout* to the *light table,* and tape a fresh sheet of paper
over it for each new page; or work in
two-page spreads as shown. For the
printer's benefit in lining up pages
on the press, mark lightly in *NRB pencil* the corners and gutters of each
page. At each step, check on the square
of your angles.

Recently, a printer I've just begun to
work with said that, since the blue lines
made by the NRB pencil do not show up on
the camera, he prefers that corners be
marked in black or red ink outside the
page. The printer is thus able to connect
the lines and determine the exact corner,
but once the page is trimmed the black
lines will not show; see the example. Ask
your printer which method he prefers.

corner

All copy which is to appear on the
page, except halftones, is then applied directly to the blank sheet.
Even blank pages, which should be labeled as such, must be represented by
a marked pasteup sheet to prevent error when the printer assembles pages
into larger sheets for *platemaking.*

154

It is most convenient to have line *graphics* prepared in the right size for your page so they may be placed at the same time as copy. Or determine the *scale* the graphic should be and have a *stat* made for the pasteup. For halftones, apply an *acetate* window, first writing in the halftone's size, identification of the picture (boy with dog) and a designation of "Photo a, p. 23" if there is more than one halftone per page. Label each graphic on the back--preferably on a stickon address label (see *illustration*) so the printer can identify and strip in each one at its proper place. (See *stripping*). The writing under the acetate window will be visible to the printer when the page is on his light table.

It's a good organizing idea to keep a running list of illustrations, the pages on which they appear, sizes and any other pertinent information, so when you're finished you have a list of the total of each type and locations; a duplicate list given to the printer may help prevent error. I also find it useful to cut all the acetate windows at once; this often reduces waste.

In fact, I do the entire pasteup on an assembly-line basis, doing each element (copy, page numbers, illustrations) separately; this means each page goes on and off the light table

4 or 5 times, which may seem like extra work--but it gives me that many
more chances to catch errors.

Copy may be fastened to the page using rubber cement or wax; other types
of glue tend to stiffen and crack,
ruining the finished page. However,
rubber cement picks up dirt easily.
After the cement is dry, lifting the
copy usually destroys it, so you must
be sure of your positioning. Because
it rolls easily and picks up smudges,
it can be removed from hands by rubbing them together and from pages by

rubbing lightly with the fingers.
Papermate (and several other companies)
put out "glue sticks" for children that
are handy for small jobs; they aren't as
messy and don't smear, but they're expensive.

I prefer wax as an adhesive, applied
with a waxer. This involves a larger
investment, but is worth it if you're
doing even one lengthy book. Or you
might borrow a waxer from your printer,
or have him wax the copy for you on
his table model; he (or you) can put
the copy through the waxer, then
place each piece on a separate, clean
sheet of waste paper so pieces won't
stick together during transport to
your pasteup center. Remember that
waxing everything in this way would
make it easier for the wax to pick up
dirt and smudges, which could be trans-

ferred to finished pages; also, excess heat will cause waxed pieces to stick to the separating sheets--which is why you place copy on them rather than putting waxed copy together. Wash your hands often with hot water when doing wax pasteup.

Copy is most easily positioned with the tip of the X-acto blade; it can be used to slide copy or to lift it for repositioning; a pair of tweezers is also sometimes useful here. Once copy is in place, put a clean sheet of paper over the page, then roll firmly over all areas with the roller or brayer. This makes the wax adhere to the paper, but copy can still be lifted and moved whenever necessary-- even weeks later. Wax never loses its adhering power, though it helps to have it slightly warm when shifting copy; turn the light table on and leave the copy on it for 5 minutes.

When doing pasteup, work as carefully and as cleanly as possible. *Camera-ready copy* is by definition clean; that is, your printer should be able to put your pasteup pages directly into his camera and make plates from the resulting *negatives* without having to *opaque* all of your errors. Any smudge, ink blot, dirty spot, will leave a white area on the negative which must be covered by hand--time-consuming and thus expensive work that you won't be there to do. You may use correction

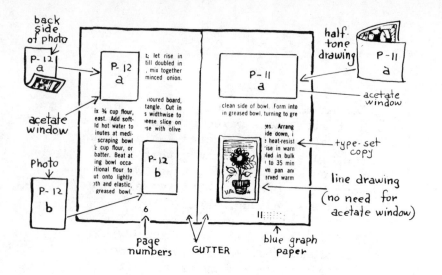

A labeled diagram of a paste-up layout showing: "back side of photo" (P-12 a), "acetate window", "Photo" (P-12 b), "half-tone drawing" (P-11 a), "acetate window", "type-set copy", "line drawing (no need for acetate window)", "page numbers", "GUTTER", "blue graph paper".

fluid in white to paint over serious
dirt spots; sometimes gentle use of
an artgum eraser works, but be sure
to wipe away all the pieces of eraser
before using *fixative*. Remember the
camera does not improve the appearance
of your work; it magnifies any errors.
When each page is finished, store in
a covered box or cupboard.

When pasting up on title pages and
other places where *display* type is
prominent, consider the effect of
white space as a positive element
in *design*. Don't crowd type elements; use a minimum of illustrative and typographic material; let
the white space emphasize the strength
of the black lettering. Notice the
contrast between the two samples
reproduced on the next two pages.
Part of the crowded effect also comes
from use of all capital letters.

A COUNTRY FOR OLD MEN AND OTHER STORIES

E. R. ZIETLOW

LAME JOHNNY PRESS

A Country For Old Men

And Other Stories

E.R. Zietlow

Lame Johnny Press

For purposes of pasteup, it is also possible to photograph and reduce an entire page. If you are using a typewriter to prepare copy, consider this approach, since typewritten copy looks better if it is about 75% of its original size. The most usual method is to do pasteup on an 11 x 14 sheet, which will be reduced on the camera to 8½ x 11.

Take special care when doing pasteup on dust jacket or cover to include not only the design elements such as title, author's name and publisher's name and/or logo, but also the *ISBN number* and *cover price*, including any extra charge for mailing. For example, if you charge $2.95 for direct sales and $3.50 mail order, both prices should appear on the jacket. Refer to sources on pasteup in Appendix 9.

Careful pasteup is essential, but don't be a slave to your layout. No matter how carefully you plan, a catalytic effect sometimes occurs during pasteup: you see combinations that you missed, perceive dimensions in the work, or ways of arranging it that open up new levels of meaning and design. Always give yourself time for pasteup to allow these little miracles to occur--rather than doing it the night before the material must be delivered to the printer.

And remember that if you were paying someone to do pasteup, you'd be paying $8 to $15 an hour.

PASTEUP TOOLS, SUPPLIES: (check italicized items in the Glossary for additional explanation):

1. *copy:* clear black print on sturdy white paper; if your copy is typeset by someone else, be sure to get 2 copies of each proof in case you damage one;

2. *graphics:* sharp, clear, good quality, for either black and white or color reproduction; not every publication requires art, of course, but consider the effect of a few well-selected items;

3. *layout* surface: opaque glass over light works best; see *light table;*

4. cutting tools: razor blades can be used for small jobs, but are awkward and dangerous after a few hours; *X-acto blades* are cheap and much easier to handle; scissors should not be used to cut copy as it's easier to get a straight line with a ruler and an X-acto knife, but you'll find other uses for them;

5. triangles: you'll need a 90-degree triangle at least 2 inches larger than the pages of your book; you might find smaller ones handy for placing illustrative material; plastic is good enough for most uses, though you'll find expensive steel ones available;

6. rulers: if you're doing more than

one publication, try to get a printer's
ruler, or *pica rule*, calibrated in
point sizes, picas and inches; a steel
ruler is handy for precise measurements, used with the triangle at all
times to keep angles square;

7. adhesive: rubber cement in small
pots with brushes works fairly well,
because spills can be rolled away,
but attracts dirt and is permanent;
sticks of glue might also work;
but for heavy use, I prefer wax, applied with a *waxer* or by the printer
in his shop; remember when transpor-
ting waxed copy to place a blank,
unprinted sheet between each 2 pieces
of waxed copy to prevent formation
of a large blob of waxed-together
copy.

8. *burnisher: for press-type*

9. roller (brayer): used, with a
blank sheet of paper to go over the
finished pasteup to improve adher-
ence; or you might substitute a
rolling pin or bottle;

10: tape: invisible tape is invalu-
able in securing edges of copy, covering press-type letters so they'll
last longer, etc. A tape dispenser
makes it possible to hold a slippery
little piece of copy with one hand
while jerking out needed tape with
the other. Double-sided tape is

useful for holding down *art,* especially if you may want to reuse it.

11. black pens: for careful retouching
of letters. Remember, the camera sees
everything, every white chip on a
black letter, so you can sometimes
touch them up--especially if you
just chipped the last Z on the press-
type sheet and it's Saturday afternoon.

12: *press-type letters:* for headlines
and chapter titles; page numbers are
also available in some *type faces* and
various sizes, as are decorative borders, architectural symbols, acetate
in various colors, and other items;

13. *nonreproducing (NRB) pencil:* light
blue does not photograph, so any marks
made on the pasteup should be made in
light blue pencil, lightly;

14. light sources: above and behind
you will help counteract light from
the table; I have several clip-on metal
reflectors with small bulbs that I
adjust pointing toward the ceiling for
bounced light, said to be more restful
to eyes;

15. waste sheets: scratch or waste paper (usually available by the ton from
your printer's floor) should be stacked
next to your light table for notes to
yourself, calculating measurements,
wiping up spilled coffee, and sundry
other uses. I also have a stack on

which I wax copy--each item is laid on
a fresh sheet of paper to be waxed,
then that sheet is discarded so that
I don't get wax on the face of the
next piece of copy to be waxed.

16. typewriter correction fluid or
opaque white ink: can be painted lightly over smudges, ink blots and most
other errors; Liquid Paper also works;
you may want to thin it, as it gets
thick and doesn't cover as well.

Some sources recommend a T-square attached to the light table; I find them
expensive and unnecessary. Also, using
one demands that your layout be taped
square to the light table, whereas if
you use a triangle it is sufficient
that the layout be square in itself.
If you do decide to get a T-square
(and self-publishing is like many other
professions in that the tools have a
certain fascination in themselves) buy
a high quality metal one; plastic,
wood and other variations are usually
overpriced and won't serve as well.
The wood ones give you splinters.

P AYMENT: most common payment schedule is to
send one third of the total estimated
cost when you send the camera ready copy
to the printer, one third when he returns
check copies to you, and one third after
the books have been shipped. This system
is fair to both parties, and gives you
some leverage should the finished copies
of the book bear any errors for which the
printer is responsible. The printer pays

for shipping and includes that cost in
your final billing, and if the books are
lost or damaged in shipment, you can
usually negotiate for compensation. If a
printer demands full payment when you send
the camera ready copy, or at any other
time before you have seen some evidence
of his work, be suspicious: ask questions,
suggest the method mentioned above. If he
won't accept it, I would suggest looking
for another printer.

P E: used to designate "printer's error" as opposed to "author's *alterations* (aa)
when proofreading.

PERFECT BINDING: see *binding*.

PHOTO COMPOSITION: see *typesetting*.

PICA: twelve *points*, about 1/6 of an inch;
pica rules, showing points, inches
and picas, are available in art and
printing supply houses, or your printer may sell you one, or hit you with
it if you ask. You may measure in
inches, but the printer will speak of
picas and points in the interest of
precision; all type is measured in
points; for example the small initial
letters in this Glossary are 24 point
Goudy Extra Bold. The pica rule is also
called a line gage.

PLATE: thin, flexible metallic sheet
from which the page image is transferred to the blanket and then to
the paper in *offset printing*; also
called an engraving.

166

PLATEMAKING: process of photographing the
pasteup, after it has been made into
a flat. Just before putting the finished pasteup on the camera, the camera man "strips in" halftone negatives
(which have been made separately by a
different process), taping them directly into the negative of the rest
of the page.

PMT (photomechanical transfer): see *stat*.

POINT: standard type measurement, used in Eng-
lish-speaking countries, referring to
.01384 of an inch, approximately 1/72;
specially made rulers measure in picas,
points and inches for each conversion.

POSTAGE: see *mailing*.

POSTERS: can be effective selling devices on
the local level; see *acetate* for ways to
make them look like expensive printed
ones. Or make them up yourself and have
them quick-printed at nominal cost.

PRE-PUBLICATION ORDERS (advance orders): often
solicited before a book appears, at
a lower price than the *cover price;*
large publishers use pre-publication
orders to test demand for a book, especially a costly one, sometimes bas-
ing number of copies printed on these
orders. While this may seem a tempting
way to obtain a downpayment for printing costs, advertising for and accepting such orders makes you legally liable for production of the book, FTC

(Federal Trade Commission) regulations require that when a customer sends advance payment, he/she is entitled to shipment by the company within 30 days. Delays require informing each customer who has sent money, giving a new shipping date, and offering to refund payment. A second delay requires automatic refund of all payments.

In addition, for a book with limited appeal, pre-publication orders may give you a false idea of potential sales, since many books sell on impulse, when the buyer sees the cover, an illustration, or is influenced by some other aspect of the actual book.

PRESS-TYPE: alphabets on acetate or polyester sheets with a pressure-sensitive coating; by rubbing on the front of the sheet with a *burnisher*, you apply individual letters to the pasteup sheet. This is the cheapest, fastest way to produce *headlines,* titles or other display type; also called: transfer lettering, run-on lettering, dry transfer, instant lettering, transfer type or pressure-sensitive type and by numerous brand names. I like Chartpak; other publishers have recommended Letra-Set and Formatt. Check art or printing supply stores and don't buy the cheapest; poor quality types are often set crooked on the sheet, are poorly designed, don't stick well and crack at temperature variations. Buy only one or two sheets at first to discover type

quality and to practice setting. You
will have to experiment with spacing
of letters to decide how you prefer
them; I place them slightly closer together than they appear on the sheets.
I also pasteup titles on a separate
sheet (often *layout paper* to keep lines
absolutely straight; once the title is
completed, I measure it and decide its
best placement on the page. When titles
are placed *flush right*, simply start
with the last letter of the word and
work to the left--but remember it's
ridiculously easy to misspell. Line
up each letter by looking along the
entire line of letters on the sheet.
Errors can sometimes be scraped off carefully with the X-acto knife and covered
with typewriter correction fluid.

Press-type has dozens of type faces,
as well as page numbers in various
sizes and rolls of tape containing
printed borders. Check your dealer's
catalog. In terms of design, I don't
recommend borders, as they soon look
cluttered. When buying, you might
want to take copies of your headlines
to help determine how many sheets
you'll need. Some faces have only
2 Y's per sheet, or 1 Z and 1 W--
and if the author's name has 6 of
each it's good to realize this in
advance. Store press-type in a cool,
dry place free of dust and don't
stack things on it.

Some examples of press-type faces
appear on the next page; see *Fototype*.

Go Chartpak's Fat Face, 36 point
Don't use fine line types like this
for stamping on covers; the lines fill
with foil ink and blur the image.

West Chartpak's Ancient Egyption,
36 point; a solid, respectable
looking type.

young Chartpak's Windsor
Outline 48 pt., a
fragile type with
its fine lines; note
breakage on y and o,
indicating type is
old and dry.

MAN! Avant Garde Medium 36 point,
with an Orbit Shaded 60 point
exclamation point.

PRESSWORK: part of the printing process involving running the paper through the
press; the 3 basic steps in printing
are *composition*, presswork and *binding*.

PROMOTION (sales): having tried both purchase of
costly ads in publications read by millions of readers and more modest, inexpensive or free forms of advertising,
I can honestly say I believe the latter is preferable in every way for the
small publisher. This experience is
confirmed by other small press people.

Basically, two opportunities for sales present themselves: pre-publication promotion, and promotion after the book is in print. Among the most important aspects of early promotion is producing an attractive product.

While you're designing the book, especially its cover, think about promotional possibilities, about how the cover itself--front and back--will help sell the book. Much of your work of promotion can be planned or completed while the book is at the printer.

Pre-publication promotion should include obtaining an Advance Book Information (ABI) form from R.R. Bowker (1180 Ave. of the Americas, NY 10036). As soon as you have a *Library of Congress* catalog card number and *International Standard Book Number*, fill out the ABI form and mail it back to Bowker. It serves as the basis for information published in *Publisher's Weekly*, *Subject Guide to Books*, *Books in Print* and *Publisher's Trade List Annual*, sources examined by every librarian and bookseller in the country-- and most of the ones out of it. These listings are free, and one of the most reliable sources of sales.

Even if you're only publishing one book, consider joining the Committee of Small Press Editors and Publishers (PO Box 703, San Francisco CA 94101; see Appendix 8 for more detail). Dues are $25 per year at this time but the monthly newsletter is a source of information on every aspect of publishing, as well as news of book fairs, cooperative distribution groups, and businesses or individuals who are dishonest or slow to pay bills. In addition, COSMEP has developed mailing lists of bookstores and libraries over the last ten years that should be the best in existence for small presses, since COSMEP is the longest-lived organization of such publishers, and since lists are edited and revised periodically, with accounts that don't pay being dropped.

Choice of a *company name* is also important even if you plan to produce only one book. Libraries and booksellers, as well as individuals, are more likely to order from a company than an individual. Consult an attorney for legal requirements for establishing a company name, which are usually simple and inexpensive. Check names in such sources as *Literary Market Place, Writer's Market,* and *The International Directory of Little Magazines and Small Presses* (App. 9) to avoid duplication. And remember to put the company name and address on the book's jacket or cover so that anyone who sees the book and wants copies can order directly from you.

Jacket promotion is popular and you may want to get some kind of advance critical comment from prominent persons or publications and incorporate it into the jacket copy. Obtain multiple copies of the manuscript, so that cri-

tical readers may examine the book
while other operations are proceeding.

Notice, for example, the book cover promotion for this book, printed either on
the book's back (if you have a paperback
copy) or the back jacket (if your copy
is hardbound). I tested the book by
using it in classrooms in South Dakota,
and the South Dakota Arts Council made
xerox copies of the rough draft for this
purpose. I asked them to send me a few
extra for review purposes, and these
were sent to a number of people important in the small press field. Some of
their responses are printed on the book.

When getting bids from your printer,
check on the cost of running extra book
jackets. These can be folded and addressed on the outside to be used for
direct mail promotion pieces, since
they carry all the information for ordering the book from you. In addition,
they can be posted in libraries, in
storefronts, or sent out as mini-news
releases, complete with illustrations.
They make striking displays if you
set up a table to sell books at a
book fair, county fair, shopping
mall or other public place. For
the price, which is usually minimal, they are an effective means
of advertising your book.

Whether your book has national or
local appeal, news releases are inexpensive and important as a source

of sales both before and after publication. Before publication, consider the various aspects that make the publication of your book actual news: the name or names of the author, especially schoolchildren, and of anyone else connected with the book; names attract readers. How is the content of the book unique? humorous? significant? heartrending? Can the release be tied to any particular season, for example by quoting a Christmas poem? Has anyone in your town ever published his own book before? Did students or amateurs construct light tables and perform other tasks that would make good pictures? Is the crochety local printer being especially helpful so that he'd make a good picture subject with the students? Be adventuresome; try to think of exciting and unusual aspects to the story.

When writing the release, put the most important or most interesting fact first, following it with the basic information about the book's origin, cost, availability. News editors cut from the bottom, so any nonessential material should be there. Include a copy of the jacket or book cover or a *stat* reduced from the original art; art of any type from a book makes stories more appealing, since any newspaper needs more illustrative material than it gets.

Reproduction of news releases is cheap and fast by *quick-print*; compare prices if you have access to several.

You could design a special news release for the book, using the title in an unusual way--running it to the right margin and down the right side of the page, for example. Or type news items on your company stationery and use quick-print to reproduce them. If you're doing a small mailing, you might want to leave the address of each copies release blank, then fill in the address on the typewriter for a more personal touch. Some companies have programmed automatic typewriters which can type the same letter over and over again, putting in a new address for each letter. After you've signed each one, they look like individually typed. I've occasionally had letters done at cost by companies having these typewriters, if they were not particularly busy.

Mailing releases is an expensive venture at best; refer to the section on *mailing* for more details. You may choose to purchase a bulk mailing permit, which reduces your per-piece postage, or you may choose to mail fewer releases and send them first class, which would make a better impression on recipients. Having tried both methods, I favor sending more pieces; also, bulk mail enables you to make several mailings to the same list for

the cost of a single first class
mailing.

After publication, you may want to send
out another batch of releases, with
the prime news element being publication and availability of the book; critical comment included with the release
is good. Remember many small newspapers
don't have the staff to write critical
reviews, so they'd rather have your review than a review copy of the book.
Again, concentrate on unusual facts a-
bout the book and its production and
think of picture possibilities: young
authors exclaiming over seeing their
work in print, for example.

Radio and television exposure, especially at a local level, is easier to
get than you might think. Call your
local station, explain the nature of
your book, and inquire about talk shows,
features, women's shows. Offer to do
readings, especially if you can persuade child authors to read for either
the TV camera or radio; cute kids can
sell anything, not to mention the automatic appeal to their parents, dozens
of relatives, music teachers and dentists. Well, maybe not dentists.

Speaking engagements and public readings are another sure way to sell. Each
service organization--Kiwanis, PTA,
church groups--has frequent dull meet-
ings and welcomes any new form of en-
tertainment or information. Kids read-

176

ing their own poems to a Kiwanis gathering, with a stack of books to sell, may be one of the best selling schemes ever devised. I need hardly mention that not only will this technique sell books, but it will help children in a variety of ways: teaching them poise, economics and something about advertising techniques.

To sell your book on a wider scale, you may want to consider book jobbers, chain book stores, commission salesmen, exhibits or large-scale advertising. For further information on these ideas, which would apply to a book with wide regional or national appeal, consult *How to Publish Your Own Book*, or *How to Publish, Promote and Sell Your Book*, Appendix 9. I don't think paid advertising or the other techniques listed return their costs, but that may not be true if you have a book with wide commercial appeal. (I publish mostly fiction and poetry, which are hard to sell in any situation). How to books are the biggest sellers today, and if you have one of these, the techniques mentioned in the sources listed might suit you. Both books have a materialistic, hard sell approach that I find displeasing, and which won't work with every book nor appeal to every author, but their advice does have some validity. Each individual must

decide how much of the technique is
appropriate for each book.

If you feel the book warrants--that
is, if it has more than local appeal--
approach reviewers for major media
publications; there is no charge
(App. 6). In order to approach these
reviewers, you'll need additional gal-
lay proofs, photo copies (which the
printer can supply at a small charge)
or a bound book. These should be
mailed to reviewers 6 to 8 weeks before publications date, with a cover
letter describing the book and giving
information about the author. Include your address, telephone number
and ordering information for the book,
as well as any critical commentary you
may already have received on this or
other work. If you get no answer, try
again, but remember these reviewers
are bombarded by hundreds of books so
try to be objective about whether or
not yours might command their attention.

Your book will also be listed, free,
by a variety of national publications;
see App. 6. Type up a sheet with the
general information most of these publications want, to keep handy for filling out forms sent to you by these
and other listing agencies that may
contact you; this includes publication
date, number and type of illustrations,
number of pages, type of binding, price
in all categories, discounts if any,
specific subject of the book (perhaps
a copy of the contents) and addresses

of any distributors who may be handling
books. These and other listing services
can help you sell a lot of books with
a minimum of effort and cost.

Three further possibilities exist for
sales: bookstores, distributors and
direct mail promotion.

Develop a good rapport with your local bookstore and take your books
directly to them, remembering that
they'll ask at least a 40% *discount*
on the *cover price*. I favor selling
books to each store at the first vi-
sit, but some will ask you to *consign*.

Since most bookstores prefer this method, you'll probably have to do it
but it's annoying and time-consuming.
Make up an invoice showing the quantity of books left, price per copy,
percent of discount and total that
the store will owe for each book, and
for all books consigned. Leave a copy
of the invoice with the store mana-
ger. Then check about once a month to
count the number of books on the shelf
against the invoice, and to collect
money. If you have good local news co-
verage, and the bookstore displays your
books prominently, you should have
enough sales to make all this bookkeeping worthwhile.

I prefer to sell to bookstores, and they
can sometimes be persuaded to buy if you
offer a larger discount, perhaps 50%, for

purchase, with a guarantee that you will buy back all books in good condition that do not sell by a certain date, usually 90 days.

An additional problem of filling bookstore orders by mail is that you know nothing of the store's quality or financial stability; you might send the third or fourth billing (by which time you've spent any profit on postage) only to receive a notice of bankruptcy or "Addressee Unknown". Publications such as COSMEP (Committee of Small Magazine Editors and Publishers) newsletter include references to bad accounts, but keeping notes on these is tedious unless you're in business to stay. The best other source I've found is Len Fulton's *American Odyssey* which lists dozens of bookstores he visited in a selling trip across the country (Appendix 9).

Distributors operate much the same way, but they are usually more organized and more capable of keeping track of where your books went, since many operate to some extent by mail. Again, a 40% to 60% discount is required, and many distributors are quite selective about books they handle; plan to send a review copy to any distributor you really want to take the book. At the same time send news releases or information about the book that might help its acceptance. Remember that entering the mail order business, whether through distributors or advertising your copies for sale in methods discussed earlier, demands professionalism in handling orders; books should go out within 48 hours of your receipt of the order, with an invoice.

My information indicates that a recognized distributor can sell your books more efficiently than you, for no more money than you would spend selling poorly. Some recommended distributors are listed in Appendix 6; you may find others in your region. Avoid those which handle primarily mass-market items, as they simply aren't interested in books that stay on the shelves for weeks and don't have full-color naked ladies on the covers. Even if you browbeat them into handling your books (which I have done) they stuff them behind *Playboy* on the racks, so you can imagine how they sell.

Direct mail promotion involves sending news releases or advertising announcements directly to customers who may buy by mail; 40% of book sales yearly result from mail order. The key to success is the quality of the *mailing list* to which you send your information; that is, does the list consist of people who will actually buy the book? This has led to great competition in creation of mailing lists, and consequent abuses, with many companies selling their lists to others, so your mailbox is always stuffed with what most of us term "junk mail." Consider carefully, first, whether your book is likely to appeal if promoted

in this fashion--and whether you want
to contribute further to such mail.
A good return from a given mailing
is 1%; I've had smaller returns. Also,
some advertising authorities agree
that people must hear or see a message
3 times before it has any effect. Consider how often you see an ad and sit
down to write a check at once--then
actually carry through to mailing it.
If you still feel direct mail is a
possibility, companies which can provide
good, inexpensive lists are listed in
Appendix 7. An example might be Resources,
which features a list of bicycle acti-
vists (whatever they are) at 50 names
for $5; a complete bookstore list, 1500
names, is $35; Massachusetts public
libraries--460--are $11. These lists
come printed on self-sticking gummed
labels for one-time use only. You may
want to enclose a return envelope with
such promotion pieces.

Philosophically, it seems to me one
of the major mistakes self-publishers
and small presses make in promotion is
trying to ape the advertising and promotion methods of major presses, the
super-hype of big business. Since the
majors have millions to spend on advertising, the self-publisher's efforts
always look cheap by comparison, especially if they use the same super-
sell language. This simply cannot suc-
ceed with today's customer, exposed to
so much advertising of a high technical

quality. Therefore the small publisher
needs to use his size as an advantage.

You published your book yourself?
How unusual! You must have learned a
lot. So use your own personality,
your own interests as a person, to
sell it. Concentrate on appealing to
the interests of individuals in your
own region. Go out among the people
you want for customers and create
opportunities for them to buy. You
need not be a high-pressure sales-
man; most of us haven't the personality for it. Just make yourself
available to the public; be friendly,
open, informative. If your book is
an example of certain skills, give
workshops as a public service--or
for a fee--and use them as a way to
sell books. Try to think of ways
you as a unique person might appeal
to other people; you can't compete
with GM on its own terms, so don't
try. Change the rules.

PROOFS: reproduction of copy after it is *typeset*; as the work progresses, they take
several forms. Galleys or galley proofs
are usually long strips with the typeset copy on them in lengths representing the amount of time the typesetter
worked. Enough space is provided on
the proof for corrections to be written at the side. Corrected or reproduction proofs are returned after
initial corrections have been noted
and made; these are sometimes termed
pasteup proofs as they are often

used in that operation. Page proofs often come in silverprint or other forms and represent the entire page after it has been pasted up and photographed; sometimes these are optional and an extra charge is made for them. Any major changes at this point will require that the page be torn up and re-photographed, an extremely expensive process, but it is wise to see these proofs.

PROOFREADING: process of checking typeset copy for errors. When typesetting you should read over what you've typed after every few lines. This will help you catch and correct many errors as you go along. But do not let this be a substitute for sitting down with the copy after typesetting and devoting your attention wholly and carefully to looking for mistakes. It is double hard to find errors in work you have written and typeset yourself--your mind tends to read the line as you meant it to look, not as it actually may appear. For this reason, it is wise, after proofreading copy yourself, to bring in someone who is not familiar at all with what you've written and who has a good working knowledge of grammar and punctuation. You might also read the copy aloud to someone who has the corrected manuscript.

Then, after you've finished pasting up the camera ready copy, reread for errors again. At this state, you can still correct errors simply by retyping the line

or word correctly. If you find an error
in the *silverprints* or check copies from
the printer, correcting it will be a
huge and expensive job.

Proofreader's symbols: similar to copyreader's symbols, except that different errors
usually occur in preparation of proofs,
and less space is available on proofs
for indicating corrections. Note also
that besides the correction in the
line, an explanation is noted at left
of the copy--never at the right. In-
line marks should be made very lightly
with NRB pencil; explanations may be
made in pen. If you do your own typesetting, you may choose not to use
these symbols, but always use them in
working with a printer. Also, in doing
your own typesetting, xerox the copy
and make corrections on the xerox, not
the original, which will become your
pasteup copy and must be kept clean.
On most typeset copy, clean corrections
can be made by retyping the correction
on another sheet of paper rather than
by using commercial correction fluids.
This is an excellent reason for obtaining a carbon ribbon typewriter for
composition; you'll catch and remove
many errors as you type.

Instruction	Symbol	Example
insert space	#	It is nowor never
close up	⌒	It is now o r never

run over to the next line	*run over*	run over. A two letter di vision should be avoided.
run back to preceding line	*run back*	run back to preceding; such division is also improper.
question of fact	*F?*	burned in 1898.
question of grammar	*G?*	Ain't got no time
query to author	*?*	Whose words these are
query to editor	*qy (ed)*	ONce upon a time
start new line	*7*	I know his house is in
Hanging indentation; all lines after first should be indented;	*hang in*	Copyreader's marks: used in the correction of manuscript copy, as opposed to proofreader's marks; these
wrong style of type	*wf*	Compositors may use vary-
set in lower case	*lc*	It is EASY TO HIT THE KEY
lower case with caps at beginning of each word	*c+lc*	Copyreader's Marks
set in roman type	*rom*	set in roman type
set in italic type	*ital*	set in italic type
delete		Publishing is hard work
insert period	*⊙*	Publishing is hard work
insert colon	*⅄*	as follows first, use

Instruction	Mark	Example
insert comma	ˏ	Henry, 92 recently
insert semicolon	;	twelveˏit was never
insert question mark	?/	Can youˏ I think
insert exclamation point	!/	You canˏ I think it will
insert apostrophe	˅	It was Joes
enclose in quotes	˅ ˅	said it wasˏhonorableˏ
insert hyphen	/-/	roughˏneck logger
insert dash	/— —/	nowˏjust in case you
reset in italics		and proofs are
reser in small caps	sm caps	and proofs are
reset in caps	Caps	Lame Johnny Press
reset in bold face	bf	Lame Johnny spoke
transpose words	tr	open a parlor massage
let stand	stet	called yesterday to say
spell out	sp	Podunk Ave is closed
begin new paragraph	¶	Hermosa is now
no paragraph	no ¶	Hermosa is no
move right	]	Yesterday he]
move left	[	[Today I can see
center on line or page	center	now is the time ctr

Following is a sample of how a piece of
copy might look after it has been proofread and marked:

Kenneth and Otto Span, a neighbr,

were hauling part of the winter's

supply of potatos from the field to

the cellar. Ottos parents had a farm

near town and also ran a hotel the

potatoes may have been for the hotel

kitchen. kenneth also did his share

of farm work; He began working on the

harrow when he was about ten. The

horses were driven, with the driver

walking behind; Wire nosebags kept

PUBLICATION DATE: arbitrary date selected by
the publisher, on which promotion begins
and books are available; the date may be
vague: "March, 1983" or specific: "March
28, 1983". Large publishers do considerable pre-publication promotion and have
often sold out the entire printing before the "publication date". In some
cases, the market is tested by giving a
special price to those ordering before a
certain date, and the publisher prints

188

only enough copies at that price to fill those orders. Based on this response, he then prints another edition at a higher price, making more profit because of lower *overrun* costs.

Q

QUICK-PRINT: shops of all types have sprung
up as new processes have been devel-
oped for fast *offset printing*. Several
variations exist, but the basis is
Itek, a self-contained process. The
copy for an Itek is photographed onto
a coated paper material that is then
placed directly onto the press; this
paper comes in a roll that "cuts itself to the right length and processes
itself, then shoots the plate out ready
to go on the press:, according to Clifford Burke's *Printing It*. Quick-print
processes are cheap, but if you compare
quality with an offset production,
you'll see definite differences. Ink is
often gray instead of black, sometimes
no attempt is made to line elements or
pages up carefully, paper may be cheap
and flimsy; some quick-printers wouldn't
recognize many of the terms in this book,
because they are businessmen, not printers.
It's a wonderful system, though, for
reproducing news releases, brochures,
other promotional items. Compare
prices and qualities, because they
vary widely.

QUOTATION (estimate, bid): all 3 terms refer to
a firm price at which printer agrees to
print your job, generally offered to
you in writing along with a set of exact *specifications* and a time limit

during which you must accept and sign
the bid or the printer will no longer
be bound by it. An estimate may also
refer to a rough calculation of how
much your book may cost, based on specs
given, but is not considered final by
the printer. If you accept an estimate
without signing anything, your final
cost may be a little higher or a lot
higher; if you are offered and accept
a written quotation or bid, you have
what amounts to a contract for the
book. Before signing, compare all bid
costs for each item of production. Where
price differences occur between printers, note whether one may have specified a lighter weight paper than you
asked for, and notice if shipping is
F.O.B. And examine sample copies of
the work from each printer before making a decision.

R

REAM: 500 sheets of paper; often available from the printer or from paper supply companies at much lower prices than the costly little packages in the stationery store; see App. 5. Paper weight, such as 20# bond, is based on weight of a ream in its full size; see *paper*.

REDUCTION: using the camera to make copy or an illustration smaller; often improves the appearance of type, especially when set on a typewriter. You must know the size the page is to be, then using a *scaling wheel* or similar method to *scale* the original down to a desired size. For example, a copy block of 4 3/4" x 7 3/4" reduces 10% to 4½" x 6 7/8", a standard size for a 5½ x 8½ book. Typewritten copy looks better if reduced to about 75% of original size; see *scaling, pasteup, typesetting*.

REGISTER: precisely superimposing in order the various colors in *color* printing or any process requiring more than one run through the press; see *four-color process*. Register marks are placed outside the print area to help camera men line up elements.

RELEASE DATE: the date on which a news release may be printed; if you are sending out releases in advance of the date the book is actually available (*publication date*) you don't want them to be printed before you're ready to ship or mail the book, so in the upper left corner type "Release date:" and the specific date on which you know the release can be printed. Leave yourself some extra time after you expect to have the books to allow for foulups in shipping and other delays.

REPRODUCTION: producing a copy of text; sometimes used interchangeably with *proof* or as repro proof, representing the copy after it has been set, *proofread* and corrected.

RETURNS: most publishers allow stores to return unsold copies for credit against future orders, provided that returns are made at least 90 days but not more than 6 months after the original purchase. The bookstore pays postage both ways, and should accompany the return with a copy of the original invoice for your convenience. A new or one-book publisher might not be able to allow returns for credit if you don't have any other books for the store to order, but you could give cash refunds. This helps bookstores accept the idea of buying books outright from you, rather than insisting on *consignment*.

RETURN ENVELOPES: see *mailing lists*.

REVERSE (flop): is a manner of creating graphic effect with little expense; a normal photo may be reversed by printing what would normally be black as white and vice versa;

the effect is striking, but little more expensive than simply printing the original photo. Type may also be reversed, producing white type in a dark area. To ask for this effect, write "reverse in margin or on the back of the graphic.

South Dakota ⒶⒶⒶ Historic Tour

REVIEW COPY (advance): a free copy of the book, often accompanied by news releases or biographical information on the author, is sent to those reviewers who are likely to actually review the book, either for a specific publication or for free-lance submission. In some cases, you might set the *publication date* far enough in advance of the date you expect to receive the finished books to allow for receiving comments from reviewers--if you consider their comment sufficiently valuable to wait for it. Or you might arrange for *galley proofs* of the book to be sent to selected reviewers so they can be reading while it's in the production process. Since galleys cost money, select the reviewers to receive them with realistic care: will they really review the book? If you work for a company with a xerox machine (or have lots of dimes) you might arrange to xerox copies of the final draft of the manuscript before typesetting, to send to reviewers.

In any case, always direct such copies to "Reviewer" rather than to a specific name, since if John Jones has left the company, your copy will probably follow him if it is addressed personally.

And always ask that two copies of the review be sent to you for your files, and for further promotion. "John Jones of *Saturday Books* says *My Friend Frances* is one of the most moving novels he has read."

Keep in mind that major publishers send out hundreds of review copies, so even reviewers for small midwestern newspapers get quantities, and it may be difficult to attract their attention to your book. Also, of the thousands of books published annually in the U.S., only about 5% get reviewed at all. Paradoxically, small press publishers get more attention than some other kinds of publishers, because there are many review journals oriented specifically to small press material, and even larger publications devote some attention to small press--since it is traditionally the advance wave of literature. See the *International Directory*, Appendix 9. Richard Morris of COSMEP suggests sending galleys to *Publisher's Weekly*, *Library Journal*, *Kirkus* and *The New York Times*, and bound books, later, to everyone else. Keep in mind that even this advice applies only if you sincerely believe that your book will impress these reviewers, or if you can afford to spend money buying galleys for a long shot. Don't spend your last dime to send galleys to *The New York Times*; spend less on regional promotion and get more results.

R EVIEWERS: large magazines and newspapers employ some writers whose job is writing critical articles on books; unless the publication is very large, the same reviewer may also cover theatre, music and several other fields. The opinions of these writers can boost sales greatly. To determine if a publication employs a regular reviewer, look it up in *LMP* or the appropriate reference for your region (Appendix 9); if the circulation is less than 10,000, chances are good no regular reviewer is employed and you might write a review of the book yourself and send it, with a news release, to the editor. If the publication does employ a reviewer, you must decide if a favorable review would be beneficial enough for you to send a copy of the book for the reviewer's opinion. In the case of medium-size publications, especially if they are not near the book's place of publication, you might send a news release with a note that you'll send a review copy if they request it.

Reviewing agencies will review a book, and in many cases send copies of the review to selected national publications, for a fee. It is a matter of individual judgment whether these agencies can actually benefit your book; publications receiving their mailings know they've been paid for the review, and sometimes disregard it for that reason. I wanted to provide more information on them for purposes of this book, but since none of them answered my letters, I'm unable to do so. That is perhaps sufficient warning.

See *review copies* and reviewers and agencies listed in Appendix 6.

RIGHTS: to a literary property, listed by *The Bookman's Glossary*: "pre-publication, serial (first serial rights); book publication, including book club; magazine second serial; newspaper second serial; book reprint; dramatization; dramatization for stock; musical comedy; amateur leasing; motion picture (commercial and non-commercial); radio; television; mechanical; electronic or xerographic reproduction, or other kinds covered in the inclusive term 'reprographic reproduction'; condensation and abridgement; anthology; translation; quotation; commercial exploitation"; most of these are commonly referred to as subsidiary rights.

RUBYLITH: see *acetate*.

RUN: print run, the number of copies produced at one time; a short run is usually 1,500 copies or fewer; see *overrun*.

RUNNING HEAD: see *head*.

S

SADDLE STAPLER: used to bind pamphlets or books
by forcing wire staples through the
middle back fold; often obtainable
at low prices, or may be operated by
the customer in some small print shops;
On ordinary book paper, most hand- or
foot-operated saddle staplers can
successfully staple through about 64
pages; larger models can handle thicker
books; see *binding*.

SADDLE STITCH: see *binding*.

SALES: see *promotion*.

SAN SERIF: see *type style*.

SASE: self-addressed, stamped envelope; should
accompany all queries to small presses
or little magazines about anything, since
few have the budget to provide postage
for all the unsolicited inquiries they
receive.

SCALE (scaling) determining finished size of
photographs or other *illustrations*,
or of entire pages, by figuring the
percentage of reduction or enlargement
from the original. I think the easi-
est method is with the *scaling wheel*,
but I'm used to using one.

Ken, my favorite quick-printer, uses
this method: on a calculator, divide
the size you want the finished picture

to be by the size it is now. If you have an 11 x 14 photo that should be 4 x 5 in the finished *pasteup*, divide 5 by 14 for 36% and 4 by 11 for 36%. If the resulting number is under 100%, it indicates a reduction; if it's over 100%, an enlargement. If the two percentages differ, take the smaller of the two and adjust the other dimension to it with the calculator.

If neither method suits you, use a ruler. First, draw the dimensions of the desired finished size of the art on a sheet of paper. Then draw a diagonal through the two opposing corners as shown. Any location on the diagonal where a vertical intersects the horizontal will be in proportion to the finished size desired. If the original art isn't in proper proportion, crop until it is. If you like gadgets,

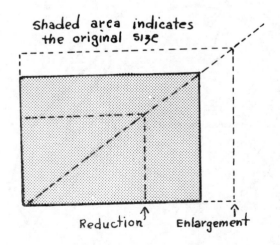

Shaded area indicates the original size

Reduction   Enlargement

Bader's (Appendix 5) has a scaleograph that performs the same function as this method but mechanically.

S CALING (conversion) wheel: a round proportional scale (or circular slide rule) used to figure proportions for enlarging or reducing *illustrations* and other elements of copy. Sizes are printed around the outer wheel and around an inner wheel, and a read out window indicates the percentage of change, which should be written on the art along with the original size. In printing, width is always given first, length second. Thus an 8½ by 11 photo is always 8½ inches wide and 11 inches long (or deep). If you wish to reduce the width of an 8½ by 11 photo to 4 inches, find 8½ on

window

the inner wheel, and turn it to 4 on the outer wheel. Then find 11 on the inner wheel and you'll see it is opposite 5 3/8 on the outer wheel; the read out window indicates the photo at those dimensions will be 47% of its original size. All of this information should be attached to the art: "photo of barn, 8½ x 11 for p. 6, a; reduce to 47%, 4 x 5 3/8".

SELF COVER: a cover of the same paper used for body of the book; not recommended since text stocks do not hold up as well as stiffer cover stocks; see *paper*.

SELF-PUBLISHING: publishing your work your own way, which you are obviously considering if you're reading this book. Unfortunately, some stigma has become attached to this practice, because some self-publishers don't bother to learn the technicalities of producing a good book. On the other hand, if you decide to self-publish, you're in good company: the company of Thomas Gray, both Brownings, Pope, Byron, Shelley, Eugene O'Neil, Tennyson, Hawthorne, Poe, Stephen Crane, Willa Cather, Walt Whitman, Thoreau, Thomas Paine and Mark Twain's boy Huck. If you still feel nervous about publishing your own work, I suggest consulting Cain's *The Co-op Publishing Handbook* and Henderson's *The Publish-It-Hourself Handbook,* Appendix 9.

SERIF: see *type face.*

SEWING: see *stitching.*

SHEET: see *page.*

SHIPPING: generally pre-paid by printer and
included in the customer's bill; see
F.O.B. Always ask how your books are to
be shipped, and ask the printer to let
you know in writing the routing of the
shipment. Most shipments will be sent by
transport truck. Small orders--1,000
books may weigh less than 1,000 pounds
and that's a small order for a trucking
company--are often shifted around on the
trailer several times, or may be left on
a dock until they can be put on a truck
going directly to your city. If you know
routing and the company or companies
that will be handling your order, you
can always trace the shipment. Transport company representatives are not always polite to people shipping small
quantities, but if you know the routing
and are polite but firm, you will even-
tually get the shipment.

I've discovered, for example, which
lines run directly from the towns where
my printers are to my own locale, and
I specify the transport firm to be used
when I am running the final check on
the book. When the printer notifies me
of the probable shipping date for the
books, and the weight, I call the local
office and describe the shipment, make
sure they have my phone number, and ask
that they look for the shipment.

Even if you live in a metropolitan area
and have an easy-to-find address, you may
find it more convenient to pick up the
books yourself, rather than wait for the
shipper's convenience. The trucking firm
will load them for you, usually packed on
a single skid, banded together with metal
strips that defy anything but tinsnips.
Inside the metal and several layers of
cardboard, the books are usually packed
in boxes of a size to be easily handled.

Some printers label each box with the number of books inside, so you have only to
check the outside of the boxes for damage
at the time you accept shipment, and open
one box to verify that they are your books.
If any serious damage has occurred, af-
fecting any number of books, you must
note that on the invoice before signing
it--or you will lose your opportunity to
hold the transport company liable. If you
are unable to inspect the shipment when
you get it, take the invoice with you,
unsigned, until you can inspect for damage.
Do not refuse the shipment (unless none
of the books are yours) because if it
goes back to the company, additional shipping will be billed to you. Once again,
with the books in your hands and 1/3 of
the final bill left to pay, you have leverage for the correction of any problems
resulting from transport.

S HOW-THROUGH: undesirable condition in which
      printing on the reverse side of a
      page can be seen through the page
      under normal conditions of light-
      ing; as opposed to *opacity*.

SIGNATURE: part of a book obtained by folding a single sheet of paper into 16 or 32-page sections; the normal unit of counting pages in printing.

SILVERPRINTS (press proofs): may be offered by a printer to show the customer the appearance of the completed book; usually consist of the completed pages made up on thinner paper than the finished book; silverprints are costly and unnecessary if you prepared your own camera ready copy or read *proofs* since silverprints are copies of the book as it has already been printed. Any change requires reprinting of the entire press run--an expensive process.

SMALL PRESSES: designation covering more than 2500 independent presses that publish a few titles a year, but generally do it with pride and quality as distinguished from *vanity publishers*; many fine books and magazines on dozens of subjects are produced by small presses yearly. Sometimes the press is created by an individual for the purpose of publishing only one book; this may lead to publishing others until, almost as a surprise, a small business is in operation. Many of these presses accept work from individuals like yourself who want a well-designed book but have little or no money; some require payment of part of the expenses, but unlike vanity presses, editors often are unpaid, or take no money until the book actually sells copies and the author has been repaid for his expense. Get *The International Directory of Little Magazines and Small Presses* or *The Directory of Private Presses and Letterpress Printers and Publishers* (Appendix 9), examine the subject entries and consider submitting your book to one of these presses. Quality varies, so always ask to see samples of their work before committing yourself. Some small presses are also *cooperative* and some do printing as a means of supporting their own press, at rates that are often far below those of commercial printers.

SMYTH SEWN: see *binding*.

SPECS (specifications): a list describing all details of the book to be published, including *trim size, number of pages*, type of *binding*, color of ink, color and weight of paper, weight of cover *stock*. This information is given to the printer as preparation for his submission of a bid.

SPINE: back of a book connecting the two covers; should give the author's last name, book title, price, and possibly publisher's name or logo and ISBN number. Everything except the number should be printed on the spine of paperbacks and the *jacket* of hardbound books. The title and/or author's name may also be stamped in gold or silver foil on the cover of the hardbound book; see *binding*.

SPIRAL BINDING: see *binding*.

SQUARE BACK: see *binding*.

STAMPING: reproducing a title, or, rarely, a design on a hard cover in gold, silver or colored foil or ink; expensive but useful especially for library editions, where the dustjacket is normally discarded for shelf display. Embossing is stamping the design or type without applying colored foil, so that the texture alone provides the decoarative aspect.

STAT (PMT, velox): positive images on photographic paper (instead of film negatives). Instead of putting acetate windows in the pasteup, and giving the line or halftone art to the printer to reduce and insert, you can take the art to him before you're ready to pasteup, have him make reductions and provide you with stats, even of halftone illustrations. Stats have slightly less detail than the original halftone, but are less expensive. Then the finished stat can be put directly into the pasteup and the entire page can be photographed as a line shot, with a reduction in steps for the printer and expense for you. This also eliminates the possibility that the printer will get the wrong illustration in place.

STITCHING: a method of holding pages or *signatures* together by means of wire staples; sewing generally refers to thread binding; see *binding*.

STOCK: see *paper*.

STORAGE: books to be kept for some time should be
placed in a cool, dry place; heat
tends to yellow even the best book
papers and dampness will rust staples
in binding and cause pages to ripple.
Shipping cartons are usually sealed
to keep out dust and moisture, so you
might leave books in cartons. Do check
shipment, however, to be sure you have
your own book and the correct number
when accepting shipment, as claims for
damages or incorrect shipping must be
made within 30 days.

STRIPPING: when pages of the book have all
been photographed, they are stripped or
taped onto sheets of paper to become
flats, pages grouped together so that
several may be printed at once. The light
blue markes placed at corners and *gutters*
during *pasteup* help the platemaker determine precise lineup of each page.

STYLE: of a book is determined by the choices
you make in determining *specifications*;
like style in clothes, style in book
design is a difficult matter to discuss.
You may prefer the extremely modern,
simple types, bright white paper, paragraphs set *flush* left, a book *jacket*
with only a dramatic splash of ink or
the title in huge, colorful letters.
Or you may want a book that resembles
an old English product, with ivory paper, elaborate *type faces*, old engravings for *illustrations* and William
Shakespeare on the cover. Whatever you

207

choose, study other books with the elements you prefer, and how the look can be altered by changing specs; see *design*.

SUBSIDY PUBLISHERS: may refer to works of specialized interest to a small group, such as a company or a community history group, which are not expected to sell to a large audience and are financed or partly financed by a grant or other funding; also referred to as sponsored books. See also *vanity publishers*.

T

TEMPLATE: plastic stencil with many sizes of
commonly used shapes and symbols, such
as circles, squares, ovals; useful if
certain shapes must be drawn frequently, or in cutting photographs to shapes.

TEXT STOCK: see *paper*.

TEXT TYPE: see *type style*.

THIRTY (--30--): used as symbol to indicate end
of a story or page, primarily in
newspapers.

THUMBNAILS: a term for rough sketches of the
job. A handy way to do thumbnails is
to take a sheet of paper the size of
the finished job and fold it into
quarters; each quarter section is pro-
portionately half the job. You can try
four versions of the *layout* of each
page in the four sections, or compare
how 2 pages will look opposite one a-
nother for balance. I like to do thumbnails of every 2-page spread in the
book, especially if it's heavily illustrated, to get a sense of how the
art and type elements will balance
one another before I start handling
the actual copy.

TRANSFER LETTERING: see *press-type*.

TRIM SIZE: one of the last printing steps, before

application of covers, is to trim all
edges of the printed sheets. The normal
trim is up to 3/8 of an inch, which
means that a 5½ by 8½ book may actually
be closer to 5 1/8 by 8 1/8 when bound.
Remember to allow for trim when doing
layout; never, for example, place important matter within a half inch or
so of the page's edge. And note in accepting *quotations* if the trim size
specified is different than your layout
for the book indicates.

Some standard trim sizes are: 4 1/8 x 7¼;
5 7/16 x 8½; 6 1/6 x 9¼; 7 5/16 x 7½ and
8¼ x 11.   Remember to allow for trim when
doing *layout*; never, for example, place
important matter within a half inch or so
of the page's edge. Note in accepting
quotations if the trim size specified is
different than your layout and specs for
the book indicates.

T YPE CALCULATION: see *copy measurement*.

T YPESETTING (composition): setting up text
material in type; may be done by hand,
by a machine which casts individual
letters or lines in hot metal (*letterpress printing*), by typewriter or other
direct-impression (also referred to
as strike-on or cold type, for *offset
printing*) and by a photographic process known as phototypesetting.

Hand set type is time-consuming even
for an expert and impractical for text

copy; however handset types are often more beautifully designed and make better impressions than other methods so you might want to ask your printer about using them for *headlines*.

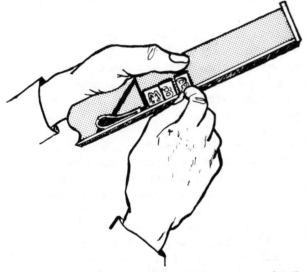

Linotype machines, used in letterpress, are rapidly becoming obsolete because of their complexity and the difficulty of finding repair parts and skilled operators. Since the weight of the type for a single page is around 10 pounds, and the type and forms for an average book may weigh over a ton, this method may be impractical for a book that requires later printings. For obvious reasons, printers don't like to store the type from one book for long; they remelt it for the next book.

Offset printing, with its use of direct-impression composition and phototype-setting, as well as its ability to use

copy produced on a typewriter, is replacing letterpress. Since anything
that can be photographed can be reproduced by offset, it's a much more versatile and efficient system than letterpress.

Variations on phototypesetting and cold
type composition exist; for further information see *Pocket Pal*, Appendix 9.
Independent typesetters from whom you
may request estimates on setting copy
are listed in Appendix 3.

Compugraphic (80 Industrial Way, Wilmington MA 01887) sells typesetting machines
of varying complexity; for the small publisher the ExecuWriter II begins at around
$4,000, carries 6 to 12 *point* text type
and produces typography in line lengths
up to 7½ inches (45 *picas*). The keyboard
closely resembles that of a typewriter,
and the machine automatically justifies
copy on the first typing, with adjust-
ments for aligning copy flush right or
left, and centering titles or headings.
There's a display window for correcting
errors before type is set, and an assort-
ment of type families are available in
roman, bold and italic. If you're in a
position to consider typesetting for
others as a way of financing your own
publishing, this is a machine to consider
first.

IBM produces a Selectric Composer which
has been purchased by some print centers
and individuals for low cost typesetting.
If there's an IBM office in your area,

ask if they've sold any of these machines locally. The composer features a variety of available type faces and sizes, justification--everything you'd want for a normal job, and usually the operators' prices seem reasonable in comparison with other cold type methods.

If you wish to do your own composition, several options exist. You can simply buy a new black ribbon, preferably the carbon type, and type the manuscript error-free. In correcting, it is best to retype the entire word or line and use invisible tape to affix it to the copy, rather than white correcting fluids; see *corrections*.

Or you may rent or buy an IBM or other carbon ribbon typewriter, preferably of the self-correcting variety. IBM's, the best and most expensive typewriter for direct impression typesetting, cost about $800 new, but may be rented for around $30 a month, with payments going toward purchase; see *IBM typewriter*.

The next few pages illustrate composition by a commercial typesetter, a typewriter without *reduction,* a correcting IBM (with which this book is being set) and hand lettering. In each case, the copy was prepared just as you see it and simply photographed by the printer; the additional step of reduction is part of the photographic process in offset printing.

in the texture of the works, he recognizes holistically the hierarchy of value structures that underlies the so often anguished worlds men design for themselves and their fellows. Nineteenth Century popular writers like Dickens deplored the "fall" represented by the post-Christian revolutions in thought while begging a return to a pastoral morality. Twentieth Century writers have frequently apotheosized the fallen state itself. They have fitted man variously to the procrustean couches of Naturalism, Freudianism, Behaviorism and Existentialism. But, going beyond these visions, Zietlow structures fall and redemption, past, present and future understanding, into a "transhominal" vision—that is, one with a holographic awareness of man.

Harold Kritze's problem is that he is trapped in the contemporary metaphysical bankruptcy of the average American while yet being tacitly aware of the next noetic rung of his evolvement. In a desperate gesture, he steps close to the brink of personal spiritual disaster in order to force (without understanding his actions) his own emergence. His behavior only reflects the true theme of his community's value level carried to its logical extreme. At the beginning of the novel then, he is paired with Kid Bennett, an avatar of that extreme. And at the end, after negotiating his passage, he is symbolically paired again.

The Heart of the Country, while marvelously comic, is similarly con-

Justified copy set in a narrow column by a professional typesetter (from a book jacket for *The Indian Maiden's Captivity/ The Heart of the Country*, a two-novel book by E.R. Zietlow, published by Lame Johnny.

214

states waited to receive the Commander-in-chief. (Military ground, this, since that day when a cloud of red dust rose from pony hoofs and the canyon below echoed to battle cries, and Sioux arrows whizzed and Cheyenne lances bickered in the sun and the buffalo grass was dyed crimson with Indian blood, a century and a half ago.) Then down the canyon again and along the shady length of River Avenue, up Eighth Street and along Chicato Avenue (once Petty's cornfield) over the Seventh Street bridge and up the winding road to College Hill (from whose crest the '86ers used to count thirteen log cabins in the town) past the white walls of the high school, and up the wide, winding highway to the Country Club, on its hilltop among the pines.

There Hot Springs served luncheon to her honored guests, and at a little distance Hot Springs' own military band played among the trees. There was no formality. High-salaried correspondents of metropolitan newspapers forgot their eternal "copy" and laughingly drove golf balls from the first tee to the velvety fairways far below, while Senators, Congressmen and even the President and his gracious lady mingled with the crowd on the veranda in neighborly familiarity. (A far cry from the rough board floors and the jungling spurs and Matt Bingham's fiddle, but the same spirit abides forever about the Springs.)

Then to the State Soldiers' Home, and a pause on the veranda there, looking down the winding gulch where Hot Springs history began and over the sweeping vista of the town--gulch and hilltop, splashes of red canyon wall and bits of lifting conglomerate cliff, masses of forest green, varying from the fresh tint of cottonwood to the black of pines. All this an Indian of old might have recotnized, but now, scattered everywhere among the hills were the walls and roofs of Hot Springs, with the great buildings of the Sanitarium gleaming on their emerald hilltop against the imposing general background of Battle Mountain.

Beauty! The befeathered, wandering savage saw it and made the canyon a shrine. Turner and Trimmer and the Pettys, drifting in from far, saw it and made the canyon a home. Evans and Jennings and Dudley and Stewart saw it and made the canyon a city. Forty years later a President of the United States, careless for the moment of the iron schedule which governs his days, saw it and lingered using his eyes. And Hot Springs of 1927, well pleased, drew away from the great man and left him alone to smoke thoughtfully as his gaze wandered across the parklike stretches of the hills, along the green slopes of the Seven Sisters and down to the walls of the little city nestled along the canyon at Battle Mountain's foot. This charmed lingering of the greatest ruler on earth might well mark the close of the first half-century of the town's history.

Copy set ragged right (see *flush*) in 12 point Adjutant on a correcting Selectric IBM typewriter and reduced to 75%; text of *The Book Book* is set in IBM's 10 point Courier without reduction. An example of this type reduced appears under *Proofreading symbols*.

my hands find trees

reaching in the dark
my hands find trees
an elm an oak a hemlock
i know them by their skins
soft leaves sharp leaves
i know them by their touch

lying on the ground
my nose smells trees
walnut hickory maple
all roots smell different
all soils smell different
i know them by their odor

standing in the sun
my eyes see trees
willow beach birch aspen
each a different green
my hands my nose my eyes
the trees speak in many ways.

from *Big Boulevard* 3:1, 1975

14

An attractive page set on a typewriter;
note its pleasing proportion in contrast
to the next page, which is also set on a
typewriter, but unbalanced. In addition,
the all-capitals type face is difficult
to read.

AND REAR SEAT WERE

FINALLY SO LOADED WITH

MILITANTS & GUARDIANS &

OTHER ANTIWAR TRASH THAT

SHE FINALLY DIED ON

WARD STREET, CORNER OF

YALE NORTH, SEATTLE,

WHICH QUEEN CITY DEMANDED

TWENTY-FIVE DOLLARS TO REMOVE

FROM WHERE WE LIVED & LIED

& LOST THE REVOLUTION

& CRIED

& FOUND A YELLOW BRICK ROAD

TO FOLLOW TO HEAVEN & JESUS

BENEATH A MASSIVE, STILTED

INTERSTATE I NEVER HITCHED ON

Each sunset is like
Opening colored stationery.
The sun taught me to sing again
When she gave me a towel
   for my tears,
And I rested for a century
Wrapped in sunsets.

My hair shouts mermaid here
more than ever before
And I didn't think anything else
could happen and it did.

from *Key West Ghosts,* 1976

26

A hand-lettered page.

ONCe UpoN a time
we were ridiNg on
a SNowfLake. The
SNoWfLake MUst
have beeN MaGiC
We hit the top of the roof
aNd NothiNG Happened.
Theday MUSt have been
MaGiC Too becAUSE it
Was SnoWiNGall
differeNt Colong.

BY Bobby
Krier

73

A page of hand composition from *thumb prints* (published in 1976 by students and teachers at St. Joseph's School, Pierre, South Dakota). The page was written by the student just as you see it, including thumbprint.

P. Wrigley

CHALLENGE

So many ways to go
   All in discord,
All with a purpose.
   All available ways a
          perposeless discord.
Making ones life an island,
Aimlessly floating about in time
          and space.

(footnote)
This was written at a time when he
was on the social security. Probably
bored and the sensational news of
the day made this reaction. In fact
he never bought a newspaper again
or listend to the news. But sa w
challenges needing attention
everywhere. But never rose to one.

from An Untitled Collection, no date

36

Copy typed on an old typewriter. A good
ribbon would have improved reproduction;
in addition, the type has not been cleaned
and the typesetter did not proofread.

Type SIZE: is measured in *points* and varies from 6 point through 10 point (most commonly used for the text of books) up through larger sizes; anything over 15 point is usually used for subheads, with 24 to 72 point used for headlines. For readability, you should not use anything smaller than 9 or 10 point for large blocks of copy. Smaller type sizes are useful for footnotes or credit lines on photographs.

6 POINT CLASSIFIED NEWS MEDIUM   Classified News is a sans-serif,

10 POINT UNIVERS BOLD   This example of Univers, a precisely defined sans-serif type

15 pt—abcdefg**ABCDEFGHIJKLM**

48 pt—ab**A**

72 pt—

TYPE STYLE (type face): type classification takes
many forms, none of which are precise.
Basically, type should be selected for
its readability: how legible it is when
arranged line after line on a page.
Many factors influence readability,
including the texture and finish of
paper, ink color, size of type and
amount of space between letters and
between lines of type.

Text types are used for most copy in a book,
the body of the book, Emphasis and variety
are possible because some styles of type
contain *bold face* lettering, and some contain
italic variations.

bted to S. Guy
g this volume.

e Publisher

text

Display types are used for subheads, titles,
headlines, in advertising, on posters--in
any capacity where a larger type size is
needed.

display

Among both display and text types, two classifications are common: serif faces have small curlicues on each letter, sometimes as small and subtle as those on the face used for this book, and sometimes more intricate, as the examples show. Serif faces vary in readability, but most book types have a slight serif.

S E R I F

Sans serif faces are more contemporary, and widely used because of their simple modern look; the letters have no serifs and are generally straightforward in design.

.u each oi
'rators and teac.
ɔating in the
the National
Office of Edu-

S A N S

Two remaining classifications are more common in display types. Cursive faces are designed to simulate handwriting; these are difficult to read even in their larger sizes and therefore not recommended for books, as the examples show.

J. Dumpling Honeyheart.

Whole Arm

Decorative faces are novelty faces used to command attention, primarily in advertising; while these may be immediately appealing, I recommend that you avoid them for books. Their extreme ornateness makes them difficult to read and could make your entire book design garish and unattractive. For more on type styles, see *Bookmaking,* Appendix 9.

TYPOGRAPHICAL ERROR: refers not to any mistakes in *manuscript* but to typesetter's errors in producing *copy*; the distinction is significant because such errors are not the customer's fault and are not charged to the customer. Errors that are your fault-- that is, which should have been corrected on the manuscript, are referred to as author's alterations (abbreviated a.a.) or customer changes; it is more costly to make alterations in copy after it has been in set in type by any method, so any corrections made at this point by the customer are heavily charged.

U

UNDERRUN: see *overrun*.
UPPER CASE: see *lower case*.

V

VALUE: refers to the degree of lightness or
of a tone of black on white, or color
on background.

VANITY PUBLISHERS: as defined in the reliable
The Bookman's Glossary (Appendix 9):
"a trade designation for publishing
concerns that specialize in publishing
books at the author's risk and expense.
They sign publishing contracts with
inexperienced authors by appealing to
their vanity or natural desire to see
their writings in print at whatsoever
the cost. They seldom have a sales
staff." Vanity publishers are sometimes, in-
correctly, also called *subsudy publishers* but
as you will see if you read that Glossary
entry, there are several important differences.
Vanity publishers also should not be con-
fused with *cooperative* publishers.

In addition, books produced by vanity
publishers are often poorly edited,
poorly designed, cheaply bound, with
unreadable type. Any promotion done
on vanity publications is usually by
badly designed brochures or advertising.
Generally speaking, publishers who
solicit your business should be re-
garded with suspicion; legitimate
publishers, even in the small press
world, don't have to look for business.

Costs of publishing with a vanity publisher vary, but remember that besides paying for all the printing costs (as you will do if you self-publish) you are paying the salaries of the people doing the jobs you could do yourself. Charles N. Aronson, a writer-publisher, lists in *A Book's Calendar* (Appendix 9) a list of 35 questions to ask of a publisher before signing a contract, to help you get what you pay for if you decide to publish by the subsidy method. They include inquiring about date of delivery of marketable copies (since one gimmick of vanity presses is to include mention of printed copies, without saying whether or not they will be bound), asking how many of the publisher's titles have sold over 500 copies (most don't) and other significant questions. Remember that the vanity publisher does not have to sell a single copy of your book to make his profit; he has it when you pay him for his services.

Don't be taken in by promotion techniques which resemble those of legitimate publishers. As a sample of the technique, consider Vantage Press' promotion for its *New Voices in American Poetry*, a title which imitates that of some legitimate anthologies, but for which authors are charged $125 per page. Editors profess selectivity: "If the editors accept my poetry, I would like my photograph included in the Poet's (*sic*) Picture Section for the additional charge of $65."

For all this cash, you receive one free
copy of the anthology in which your work
is published--additional copies must be
purchased, further enhancing the profits
for Vantage. Remember, the company has
already made enough money by the time the
book is printed so that they would not
need to sell a single copy to receive
a profit. But to make their offer seem
more legitimate, the company lists some
libraries and review publications that
will receive copies of the book, including the *Chicago Review, The New York
Times, Washington Post.* I think I can
assure you that had any of these publications actually reviewed the book, the
reviews would be quoted.

Well-known vanity publishers include the following: Dorrance and
Company, Exposition Press, Mojave
Books, Vantage Press and William-
Frederick Press. Some (but not all)
vanity publishers are listed in
Writer's Market. See also *cooperative publishers, small presses,
subsidy publishers.*

VARNISH: a type of wax applied over the outside
covers after printing, to add a glossy
finish and increase durability for paperbound books; usually included by
printers as a regular service, but if
it isn't mentioned in the *quotation,*
ask about cost, as it adds to the attractiveness, durability and professional
appearance of your book.

V_{ELOX}: see *stat*.

WASHUP: cleaning a press to change ink color; see *color*.

WAXER (wax coater): a machine that applies wax to back of copy so that it will adhere to *pasteup*; several varieties of varying complexity exist; printers may have a small table model with which they will wax your copy, or allow you to wax it, to take home for pasteup. Copy to be transported waxed should be separated by sheets of scrap paper.

However, if you are doing a large book, or more than one book, you'll want a hand waxer, which can be plugged in beside your light table 24 hours a day without using much electricity, can wax large pieces of copy as well as small ones (which sometimes disappear into the maw of a table waxer never to be seen again) and will pay for itself within a few pages by saving frustration. Small bars of wax are put into the back of the waxer, where they melt and run down onto the roller. When you roll it over the back of a piece of copy, wax is distributed evenly over the surface. Use only wax made for the machine; any other type will gum it up. Bader's catalog, listed in App. 5, features waxers and wax for reasonable prices. (Sketch on next page).

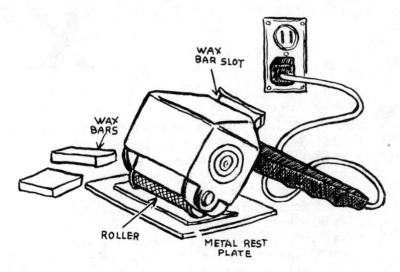

WAX
BAR SLOT

WAX
BARS

ROLLER

METAL REST
PLATE

WIDOW: in copy, a single word in a line by itself ending a paragraph or page, or beginning a page; strict typesetters
frown on such sloppiness and may call
it to your attention if you set your
own *copy*. Referred to as a bad break
if it appears in *pasteup*; even though
most readers won't be bothered by it,
your work looks more professional if
you avoid such things; note the one on
page 230.

WINDOW: see *acetate*.

X

X-ACTO KNIFE (Exacto): a razor-like blade
(in some older models an actual razor
blade) with a twist mechanism (called
a chuck) permitting you to change
blades when the old one gets dull;
used for cutting copy during *pasteup*;
such a knife cuts more accurately and
safely than a razor blade alone, and
with less strain on the hand; used
for various hobbies as well as in art
and may be cheaper in a hobby store.
If they haven't been nicked or
chipped, blades can be sharpened
for longer use by rubbing them
over a piece of glass, or over any
whetstone.

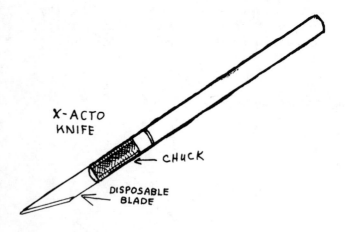

X-ACTO
KNIFE
← CHUCK
DISPOSABLE
BLADE

Appendices:

The material in the following appendices has been selected from volumes
of information that I've collected--
or that has accumulated around me--
over the years. I've annotated sources
I've used, and included those I consider most useful to someone beginning to publish. I've also mentioned sources I think are dread-
ful to keep you from relying too
heavily on them.

Remember: you can publish a book
with the information in the pre-
ceding pages. That which follows
will add to your knowledge; but
during the time you're researching,
you are not publishing. If you
really intend to publish, get at
it. Look for these sources (instead
of chewing your fingernails) when
your printer has one of those
"unavoidable delays" mentioned in
the fine print.

Words which were italicized earlier
so that you would look them up in
the Glossary are no longer set apart;
this is a kind of "final test" of your
new vocabulary.

Appendix 1:

Flow Chart

Remember that many of these jobs overlap; you may be typesetting while you
type the final draft of the manuscript.
You can send for copyright forms as
soon as you begin planning the book,
but Library of Congress forms require
that you give information on the
format. Continually refer back to
Glossary entries for details on each
of these steps. You might want to
construct your own flow chart with
appropriate entries so you can keep
track of completion of each step.

JOB: IF COMPLETED   DATE

Manuscript preparation

    typed
    facts checked
    copyread
    final draft typed
    typeset

Format selection:

    trim size
    page design
    page arrangement
    text stock

```
          type styles: text
                       headlines
          number of copies
          paperbound: perfect bound?
                      saddle stitched?
                      other?
          hardbound:  grade of cloth?
                      stamping?
          cover price
          overrun jackets?
Art:

    cover art: chosen
    checked with printer
    dummied
    pasted up

    text illustrations: chosen
    checked with printer
    stats made?
    pasted up

Copyright:

    information requested
    form completed, fee sent
    copies deposited

ISBN number:

    information requested
    designated
    placed on pasteup

Library of Congress number:

    information requested
    received or denied
    placed on pasteup
```

236

Promotion:

    news releases written
    releases copied
    publication date set
    releases sent
    public appearances arranged
    orders: invoices designed
                      printed

Typesetting:

    begun
    completed
    proofread
    corrected
    proofread
    corrected again

Layout:

    completed

Pasteup:

    completed
    checked

Platemaking:

    page proofs checked

Printing:

Folding:

Collating:

    can you help?

Binding:

Books received:

    date placed on display or sale
      for Copyright records

Don't forget that expenses for all
phases of publishing your book--from
buying paper and ink through trips to
the printer's office--can probably be
deducted from your income taxes. Consult an accountant for details.

And keep careful records of sales,
also for income and other types of
tax records--including whether the
purchase was by an individual or an
institution, how much was paid, and
postage costs.

For more information, ask for applicable
publications from the Internal Revenue
Service, 1111 Constitution Ave., Washington,
DC 20224.

Appendix 2: Bids

Reproduced on the following pages is a selection of bids received on *The Book Book*. For practice, compare the various specs, services and charges and see why I chose Town House Press (see page 247).

Once you sign a quotation indicating your acceptance (you normally have 90 days to accept the bid before the price ceases to be binding on the company) you have entered into a contract to publish your book with that company. Some contracts specify that even if you cancel your publishing plans, you must pay the printer for everything he has done until the day of cancellation.

Other conditions usually include: that overruns or underruns not to exceed 10% shall constitute acceptable delivery; that the contract is subject to strikes, riots, warfare, government laws or regulations, available materials and conditions beyond the control of the printer. Translated, the latter means that if practically anything happens to your book while it is in the hands of the printer, he is not responsible. Never send a manuscript, pasteup or anything else anywhere without keeping a copy of it.

9-18-78

L.M. Hasselstrom
Lame Johnny Press
Box 66
Hermosa, SD 57744

Dear Mr. Hasselstrom:

Please find enclosed our bid for your book of 112 pages, 1500 copies.
I have also enclosed a copy of a book we recently printed with all line
copy, as the sample you have requested.

Your books would be shipped to you via trucker, which means you would
have to supply us with a street address to which they could deliver.

Our payment procedures are as follows. We require a 50% deposit with
the order. When the books are completed, we will send you a copy for
your inspection, along with an invoice for the completed book.
When we receive the balance of payment from you, your books will be
immediately shipped, and you should receive them in 4-5 days.

The books would take about 12-15 working days to process at our plant.
This assumes that you notify us 2-3 weeks in advance of sending your
copy so that we can schedule your work. If you send the copy to us
without prior noticiation, it may take 4-5 weeks to complete your books.

Please do write again if you have any further questions. We hope we'll
be doing business with you soon.

                                        Yours truly,

Date: 9-18-78

.L.M. Hasselstrom
.Lame Johnny Press
.Box 66
.Hermosa, SD 57744

Dear Mr. Hasselstrom:

We are pleased to offer you the following quote on your book.

TITLE _____unknown_____ QUANTITY ___1500___

TRIM SIZE: 8½x11____ 5½x8½ xx 7x8½____ Other_____

NUMBER OF PRINTED SIDES:__112_____ NUMBER OF LEAVES (excluding covers) _2

ILLUSTRATIONS: Line art___yes_____ Halftones (describe)_____none_____

PAPER (WE SUPPLY): 50# white_xx Other_____

INK: Black only unless other arrangements are made

CAMERA READY COPY: Yes_xx No____

COVERS: We supply_xx Customer supplies____
         67# Vellum bristol____ Other_xx 10 pt. coated one side
         Cover ink: Black only_xx Special____
         Camera Ready: Yes_xx No____
         Other information:

BINDERY: 3-stitch_____ 3-hole Drill___ Other_____
          Saddlestitch____ Brads?_____ _____
          GBC_____ Holland Tape___ _____
          Perfect binding_xx Color?_____

OTHER OPERATIONS NOT INCLUDED ABOVE:

                    * * * * * * * * * *

Number of copies   1500   _____   _____

Text: platemaking, printing,
   collating   858.00

Cover printing (may increase if ink   250.00
                coverage is heavy)
Binding   450.00

Subtotal: 1558.00

Per book cost: 1.0387

Additional charges for special operations:
   One time setup charge: 33.00
   Shipping (est.)   90.00
TOTAL CHARGES: $1681.00   _____   _____

Prices subject to revision after 30 days.

L.M. Hasselstrom
Lame Johnny Press

L.M.:   Re: <u>The</u> <u>Book</u> <u>Book</u>

Thanks for your inquiry.
(I know your work - <u>Homegrown Poems</u> - I'm a teacher and
once purchased your book).

Anyway, now that I'm trying to get this new business off
the ground, I'm quite sure that I can do your book, 1500
copies, 112 pages, perfect bound, for $1500.

As to your questions:
No we don't do casebinding.
Shipping and payment procedures: We'd like 2/3 up front/
1/3 after delivery.(We're small guys with our own new and
fluctuating overhead concerns.)We'll ship special handling.

Our coated stock is white only. Is that OK?

September 14, 1978

Lame Johnny Press
Box 66
Hermosa, SD 57744

Gentlemen:

Thank you for your interest in our book printing service. The
enclosed catalog and price list will give full details as well
as cost of producing various size books in different quantities.

The cost of printing your book will be as follows:

    1500 copies, 112 page 5½x8½ book, printed by   *974.40*
        offset on 50# white paper @ $ 8.70 per page $ ~~974.40~~

    kromekote covers - black ink 10 pt.-perfect bound   135.00

         Total cost of order - postpaid   1109.40

Note that the above price includes prepaid delivery to any one
address in the United States. Production time would be from 45
to 60 days. Terms for offset printing are payment in full with
order.

We know that you will be pleased with our work and service and we
shall look forward to working with you in getting your book into
print.

                     Sincerely yours,

JG:ss

November 28, 1978

Mr. L. M. Hasselstrom
Lame Johnny Press
Box 66
Hermosa, South Dakota 57744

Dear Mr. Hasselstrom:

This is surely a long delay in responding to your note of September 9, 1978, in which you outlined specifications for a title identified as: THE BOOK BOOK.

I assume most of your publications are now printed via sheet-fed offset. Unfortunately, this is an area in which we do not compete. Our greatest strength falls in the area of long-run web offset printing. However, we also have a separate production facility in which we operate several Cameron Belt Presses.

The Cameron Belt Press is unusual in that it creates a book as a single in-line operation, including the binding and trimming. Perhaps 70% of the books we print on this equipment are paper covered; the balance 30% are covered with the endsheets and then cased-in.

I am including some descriptive material on this equipment. If it appears of interest, I will be glad to answer further questions or discuss projects with you for future production.

Although I am sure you have already placed your order for THE BOOK BOOK, you might want to note that our manufacturing prices based on a quantity of 2,500 copies (which is our minimum quantity for book work) would have been as follows:

    Text film from your reproduction proofs - $178.00

    Estimated cover film   - $ 80.00

    Text plates, one-time charge   - $145.00

    Manufacturing price, which includes paper stock, presswork,
    binding and packing -

        2,500 copies   - $1,195.00
        Additional thousands -   175.00

You will note I have quoted the film and plates separately, since these are one-time charges. The manufacturing price represents a first printing price as well as current reprint price.

Incidentally, in the trim size you have specified (5-1/2" x 8-1/2") the Belt Press delivers in 12-page units; thus, the prices I have quoted are for a book of 108 text pages. The next step to a larger account would be 120 pages, at slightly additional cost for the film, plates and manufacturing.

Please don't hesitate to call if you have questions or need further information.

My best wishes.

Sincerely,

FKP:vc

Date   September 18, 1978

Estimate #90109

Representative

To: Linda Hasselstrom
LAME JOHNNY PRESS
Box 66
Hermosa, S.D.   57744

We take pleasure in submitting this quotation to you. It is based on the following specifications and this quotation will remain in effect (unless otherwise specified in writing) for a period not to exceed 120 days.

Title:_____ THE BOOK BOOK _____

Pages__112_____ Trim size__$5\frac{1}{2}$ x $8\frac{1}{2}$__ No. of copies__2000 - 1500 perfect/500 case

Composition:	None
Paper:	Text - 50# White Cover - 10 pt. White Carolina Dustjacket - 80# White Enamel
Plates:	Made from camera ready copy
Printing:	Text - printed black ink throughout Cover - printed black one side plus varnish Dustjacket - printed black one side plus varnish
Binding:	Perfect and smyth sewn, cased into A grade cloth over binder's boards, head bands, white end leaves, foil stamping on the spine. Dies additional, apply dustjackets.
Packing:	Bulk pack in cartons
Tentative Schedule:	

Total price____$1,594.00____

Terms_Subject to credit o.k.

F.O.B._____Ann Arbor, MI.____

P. O. No._____Date_____

246

February 19, 1979

Ms. Linda Hasselstrom
Lame Johnny Press
Box 66
Hermosa SD 57744

Dear Ms. Hasselstrom:

We thank you for the privilege of re-quoting THE BOOK BOOK, in accordance with the following specifications:

5 1/2 x 8 1/2, 344 pages, printed in black ink on 50# white text. Paperback edition to be covered in 10 pt. Coated cover, printed one color and varnish, perfect bound. Casebound edition to bound in C Grade cloth with single stamp on spine.

Dust jackets, if desired will be one color and varnish on coated stock, wrapped on books.

Total print run for this title to be 1500 copies.

To print, bind and deliver 1500 copies all paperbound the cost would be $1.69 per copy...$2535.00

To print, bind and deliver 1200 paperbound copies and 300 casebound copies, the cost would be:

      1200 paperbound copies @ $1.72...$2064.00
      300 casebound copies @ $2.70...$810.00
                                  $2874.00

Additional hit on casebound cover or spine - add $.07 per copy.

One color dust jackets, including wrapping - add $.78 or $234.00.

Terms on this title would be one-third deposit, one-third 30 days after shipment, balance 60 days after shipment.

Delivery time would be 5 to 6 weeks for paperback edition, 10 to 12 weeks for casebound edition. Sample C Grade cloths are enclosed. All material from you to be camera-ready.

Good luck with your publishing ventures.

Taxes and transportation charges are not usually included in quotations; terms of payment are usually 30 days with a service charge for late payment, and the purchaser usually agrees to defend the printer against any suit brought as a result of material printed in the book. All these conditions are standard.

What you should guard against are provisions requiring you to pay in full when sending copy, as specified by the bid from Adams Press, for example. To pay before seeing any of your book leaves you no leverage should you be dissatisfied with production. While this or any company requesting such payment might do excellent, honest work, I'd still advise you not to close your doors in that manner. Suggest paying one third when you send copy, one third when you check proofs, and one third upon shipment. If the company won't accept that, look for a smaller company. This is a case when use of a company name might help.

Another thing to watch for is shipping charges: are they included in the original price, or will they be added? If you budget just for the printing price, $100 in shipping charges could be a shock.

Appendix 3: Services

Typesetters:

Write individual companies for information based on your particular needs.

East Coast Print Center
Box 1050
Brooklyn NY 11201

Specializes in work for small presses.

West Coast Print Center
1915 Essex St.
Berkeley CA 94703

Likewise; both funded by grants, non-profit; both shops also do printing for literary magazines and small presses only--remember you are a small press if you give yourself a company name. Both print centers can probably print and bind more cheaply than the volume printers listed in Appendix 4 on saddle-stitched and other small books in editions of 1,000 or less. But for a perfect bound or hardbound book, or for more than 1M copies, check with the larger printers. Get bids from several sources and compare.

Northwoods Press, Inc.
RFD #1
Meadows of Dan, VA 24120

Fast, efficient, friendly, inexpensive,

excellent typopography and printing;
write for information and type styles.
Northwoods requires apprixmately one-
fourth of the expected typesetting cost
as a deposit, and works on a schedule of
20-25 pages per day, so you know when
your copy will be completed. This is a
real advantage, since some compositors
put off small jobs for larger ones.

Holographics
1623 10 Ave.
San Francisco CA 94122

Independent Type Service
Box 292
Pierre SD 57501

Owner Nan Steinley has an IBM Composer
with a variety of type styles, and
guarantees to deliver copy without
error at reasonable rates.

Pacific Sun
21 Corte Madera Ave.
Mill Valley CA 94941

San Serif Typesetters
2378 E. Stadium
Ann Arbor MI 48104

Morty Sklar
PO Box 1585
Iowa City IA 52240

Morty is a small press publisher,
takes great pride and care with

typesetting, promising it error-
free.

Sherrell Graphics
333 S. Van Ness Ave.
San Francisco CA 94103

What's Your Line Graphics
964 Valencia St.
San Francisco CA 94110

Also see Appendix 4, since some volume
printers, and many smaller printers,
also do typesetting at reasonable
rates.

Sources of Illustrations:

Local artists, art students

Call high schools and colleges for names
of students who might want to earn a
little extra money by providing the
art you need, or who might work free
to have their names on your book.

Newspapers

Check with your local paper for
discarded art books which are purchased in quantity for advertising
production, and often thrown away
when the new book becomes available.

U.S. Government

An excellent source; for example, ask
your local Agricultural Stabilization
and Conservation Office for government
sources if you need pictures of apple
trees, or diagrams of methods of fer-
tilizing; the Forest Service could
direct you to pictures of bald eagles.
For practically every subject, there
is a government agency so take advantage of it.

Organizations

If you need pictures having to do with
a particular field, especially a very
specialized one, write to the organi-

zation of professionals. A reference librarian, or some of the reference sources in Appendix 9, can help you discover the appropriate organization.

"Pictorial Archives"
Dover Publications
180 Varick St.
New York 10014

A group of books published for anyone who needs art for reproduction; when you buy a book, you buy full rights to reproduce any of the material therein without further payment or acknowledgement; includes such titles as: *American Indian Design and Decoration, Montgomery Ward Catalogue of 1895, Curious Woodcuts of Fanciful and Real Beasts, The Book of Monograms and Alphabetic Devices, Dictionary of American Portraits, An Old-Fashioned Christmas in Illustration and Decoration, and Games and Pastimes of Childhood*; an opportunity to obtain professional art without much money.

Museums, Galleries

If you have seen reproductions printed elsewhere that you want to use, note in the credit line where the original painting is, and write the museum or gallery, explaining the use you want to make of the painting. Many museums, according to Richard Morris of COSMEP, are more interested in the publicity your use might give them than in a fee. Some may send good photographs. If

they do charge, it's usually on a
sliding scale: more for a cover, more
for color reproduction, more if the
painting is to be used in an advertisement.

"Picture Sources"
Writer's Market
9933 Alliance Rd.
Cincinnati OH 45242

Annotated list; most of these sources
charge, however, from $25 to several
hundred dollars.

Harry Volk Art Studio Catalog
Box 4098
Rockford IL 61110

Free; offers 244 books of line art on
a variety of subjects for use in books;
books are described in the catalog.

Instant Art for Direct Mail and Mail Order
Career Publishing Corp.
PO Box 19905
Dallas TX 75219

Labels, slogans, symbols for advertising
and promotion.

Bettman Archive
136 E. 57th St.
New York 10022

Culver Pictures
660 First Ave.
New York 10016

> Companies which specialize in supplying
> pictures for various uses, and do charge
> fees, often high ones if the picture is
> rare. Both have sliding scales of charges,
> so describe your needs and ask for an
> estimate of costs. The company supplies
> photocopies and price lists, and you pay
> only for what you use.

Editing by Design: Word-and-Picture
Communication for Editors and Designers
Jan V. White
(New York: Bowker, 1974)

> Besides being one of the best sources
> around on how to use illustration, the
> book lists some accessible sources of
> illustrations.

Papermakers:

Andrews Nelson Whitehead
3110 48th Ave.
Long Island City
New York 11101

The Bieler Press
4603 Shore Acres Rd.
Madison WI 53716

Crestwood Paper Co.
26 Cypress Ave.
Mill Valley CA   94941

Crestwood Paper Co.
315 Hudson St.
New York 10013

Farnsworth & Serpa
1333 Wood St.
Oakland CA 94607

Flax's
250 Sutter St.
San Francisco CA 94101

Matagiri Paper
Mt. Tremper NY 12457

Mere Cie
6455 Geyser Ave.
Reseda CA 91335

N.Y. Central Supply Co.
62 3rd Ave.
New York 10003

NovaDreadnaught
PO Box 187, Bear River
Nova Scotia, Canada

Twinrocker, Inc.
RFD #2
Brookston IN 47923

Part of this list appeared in an article in
Type and Press, Summer, 1977, No. 13, and was
brought to my attention by Dwight L. Musser,
a publisher at Box 305, Ridge Manor, FL 33525

Bookbinders:

If you deal with a volume printer, the company already has binding facilities, or a standing agreement with a bindery, so you need not be concerned. You might ask who does their binding, and do ask to see a sample before closing the agreement. If, however, you have your book printed locally and the printer can't do the type of binding you prefer, check the listings in *LMP* under Book Manufacturers. At the end of that classification are entries on different phases of publishing, with manufacturers that specialize in different phases of publication.

Mrs. Gerhard Gerlack
The Bookbinders Workshop
The Old Mill
Shaftsbury VT 04562

Stanley Clifford
Deer Isle ME 04627

William H. Dierkes
Box 509
Eureka Springs ARK 72632

R.R. Donnelly & Sons Co.
The Lakeside Press
2223 Martin Luther King Dr.
Chicago IL 60616
Graphic Conservation Dept.

Dreadnaught
24 Sussex Ave., Toronto
Ontario, Canada

Lo Gatto Bookbinding
396 Patterson Ave.
East Rutherford NJ 07073

Ernest Hertzberg & Sons
Monastery Hill Bindery
1751 Belmont Ave.
Chicago IL 60657

Carolyn Horton & Assoc.
430 W. 22 St.
New York 10011

Various individuals also do hand binding;
see *Literary Market Place* and watch the
COSMEP Newsletter for announcements.

Appendix 4: Printers

Volume Printers:

All of these printers specialize in
short run printing (1-5,000 copies) of
perfect bound books, and on such
specs can underbid even the grant-
supported print centers listed in
Appendix 3. Also, the companies are
familiar with the problems of con-
ducting business by mail and telephone.

Banta
Curtis Reed Plaza
Menasha WI 54952

Banta has several divisions, depending
on your area; for information contact
the address above. Plants are located
in Wisconsin and Virginia, with sales
offices in New York, New Jersey, Washington D.C., Massachusetts, Illinois,
Ohio, Wisconsin and California. Because
the company has a high-speed belt press
system, your book progress very quickly
from a roll of paper to a book, enabling
the company to give excellent prices on
large quantities; that is, above 2500
copies on a book of 100 or more pages.

Braun-Brumfield
Box 1203
Ann Arbor MI 48106

> I've done several books with B-B, and
> found the company conscientious, in-
> expensive, high-quality; when an error
> was made, it was quickly corrected at
> company expense without a quibble and
> employees are careful to check any
> questionable matters with me before
> proceeding.

Cushing-Malloy, Inc.
1350 N. Main St.
Ann Arbor MI 48107

> I've worked with this company through
> Town House Press, and it does fine,
> reasonably priced work.

Edwards Brothers
2500 S. State St.
Ann Arbor MI 48104

> According to Len Fulton of Dustbooks,
> Edwards is 10-15% higher than Braun-
> Brumfield and Lithocrafters, but does
> an excellent job.

Lithocrafters
Box 1266
Ann Arbor MI 48106

> Highly recommended by other small press
> publishers for high-quality, low cost
> work.

Malloy Lithographing
5411 Jackson Rd.
Ann Arbor MI 48104

> Karl Pohrt and David Robbins of Bear
> Claw Press said to contact Robert
> Schieble at Malloy; that they've been
> delighted with the work done for
> them by this company.

McNaughton & Gunn
PO Box 2060
Ann Arbor MI 48106

> Highly recommended by small press
> publishers for high-quality, low cost
> work; has occasionally refused to print
> "objectionable" graphics.

The Town House Press, Inc.
28 Midway Rd.
Spring Valley NY 10977

> All aspects of production for small
> presses, and will give advice on sales
> and publicity; Alvin Schultzberg, pre-
> sident of the company, takes an inter-
> est in all books produced, even calling
> to suggest changes in design if he's
> convinced you've made an error--and
> he's a positive nit-picker on errors,
> which is the kind of service I like.
> For this reason, Town House printed
> *The Book Book*.

Adams Press
30 W. Washington St.
Chicago IL 60602

> Also does typesetting, binding, and
> production of book jackets as separate
> processes from book publishing; demands
> full payment before work begins, but
> if you're having them do only a seg-
> ment of your book, you might not mind
> the risk.

R.P. Donnelly & Sons
2223 King Dr.
Chicago IL 60616

> Reported to do excellent work.

Other Low-cost Printers

North Country Anvil
Jack Miller
Box 37
Millville MN 55957

> Beginning with his own down-home
> publication (the *Anvil*) Miller has
> collected friends/assistants and
> equipment until he's able to do
> excellent work on short run books
> at competitive prices. Query with
> an SASE and if you have any interest
> in the culture and crafts of the
> middle west, both past and present,
> as well as history and current affairs
> from the region, enclose $5 for some
> back issues of the *Anvil*--lively
> reading.

California Syllabus
1494 MacArthur Blvd
Oakland CA 94602

> Produces small, no-frills editions
> from camera-ready copy quickly and
> reasonably; specializes in academic
> work; write for the company publica-
> tion *How to Make a Book* for specific
> requirements

East Coast Print Center
Box 1050
Brooklyn NY 11202

The Graywolf Press
Scott Walker
PO Box 142
Port Townsend WA 98368

      Has produced some excellent work;
      query with an SASE as they may have
      all the work they can handle.

Lorrah & Hitchcock
Publishers, Inc.
301 S. 15th St.
Murray KY 42071

      Send for the company's booklet,
      Publish Your Book Your Way, to learn
      about their low-cost methods; prices
      seem to be reasonable.

Northwoods Press, Inc.
RFD #1
Meadows of Dan VA 24120

Morty Sklar
PO Box 1585
Iowa City IA 52240

West Coast Print Center
1915 Essex St.
Berkeley CA 94703

Wampeter Press
Box 512
Green Harbor MA 02041

>   Recommended by small press publishers;
>   samples show the company does excellent
>   work; promises to underbid most other
>   printers

>   For further information, look for
>   printers listed in these sources,
>   which should be in the library.

Book Publishers Directory
(Gale   Research Co.
Book Tower
Detroit MI 48226)

Guide to Women's Publishing
Women Writing Press
RD 3
Newfield NY 14867

*International Directory of   Little Maga-
zines and Small Presses*
Dustbooks
PO Box 1056
Paradise CA 95969

Literary Market Place
R.R. Bowker
1180 Ave. of the Americas
New York 10036

Directory of Private Presses and
Letterpress Printers and Publishers
1978, $5
Press of Arden Park
861 Los Molinos Way
Sacramento CA 95825

> As I was completing this appendix, it
> occurred to me that one source I had
> not found was a guide to those smaller
> printers who are willing and able to
> handle production of work from other
> writers. Some are listed in the *Inter-*
> *national Directory of Little Magazines*
> *and Small Presses,* but they're not
> categorized separately so they're hard
> to locate. Then my January, 1979 issue
> of *Small Press Review* arrived, and the
> review section carried a listing for
> this book.

> The directory contains 305 listings of
> letterpress printing/publishing opera-
> tions in the world, with equipment,
> type faces available, kinds of work
> produced, willingness to exchange with
> other presses, and goals and philosophy
> of each press.

American Publisher's Directory
K.G. Saur Publishing
175 5th Ave.
New York 10010

> First published in 1978, the directory
> lists over 25,000 publishers, with
> areas of specialization, addresses,
> telephone number and ISBN publisher's

prefix. The directory appears to be
directed primarily to book merchants
but would be useful to writers looking
for a publisher since it lists those
whose yearly production may be fewer
than 5 books.

Appendix 5:

Printing Supply Houses

Tools I've mentioned may be ordered through these firms; many offer free catalogs, or refund purchase price with your first order. You can learn a lot about printing and design just by looking at the catalogs. Do compare prices, as they vary greatly, but prices from these suppliers are always lower than from office or art supply stores, though you have to buy without examining the tool. You may not need a company name to order from these companies, but if you have one, you might be elgible for discounts.

Aldy Graphic Supply, Inc.
1115 Hennepin Ave.
Minneapolis MN 55403

> Dealer for Chartpak press-type lettering; ask about dealers in your area.

Bader's Art Supply
1113 Locust
St. Louis MO 63101

> I order everything from this supplier; a clearly explanatory catalog and good, inexpensive tools. Dealer for Letraset and Zipatone transfer lettering, and Grumbacher artist supplies.

Compugraphic Corp.
80 Industrial Way
Wilmington ME 01887

> Computer controlled photo typesetting
> equipment; see *typesetting*.

A.B. Dick
5700 Touhy Ave.
Chicago IL 60648

> Printing and binding equipment; write
> for the name of your local dealer.

Gaylord Bros.
Box 61
Syracuse NY 13201

> Book binding supplies.

Goldsmith Bros.
670 Dell Rd.
Carlstadt NJ 07072

> Hand operated saddle staplers, files,
> gathers for collating, table paper
> cutters, office supplies.

Goldsmith Bros.
141 E. 25 St.
New York 10010

> Writers can buy paper, folders, type-
> writer ribbons and other office supplies,
> as well as small copiers and other
> office machinery at low rates.

Letraset
2379 Charleston Rd.
Mountain View CA 94040

Letraset
33 New Bridge Rd.
Bergenfield NJ 07621

      Write the one closest to your area;
      suppliers of press-type lettering and
      graphic art supplies; send for a free
      catalog.

The Kelsey Company
Meriden CT CT 06450

      Supplier of printing presses, type
      supplies, paper and other machinery.

Michael Business Machines
145 W. 45th St.
New York 10036

      Printer's cutters and other machinery.

AM: Multilith Division
1800 W. Central Rd.
Mt. Prospect IL 60056

      Printing and copying equipment.

Pickett Industries
17621 Von Karman Ave.
Irvine CA 92705

      Templates, lettering guides, triangles,
      t-squares, curves, drafting tables,
      drawing instruments and accessories.

Quality House, Inc.
PO Box 252
Oakland Gardens NY 11364

> Supplier of stationery, office
> supplies, legal forms, printing,
> engraving and artists' materials
> and office furnishings.

Swingline
Long Island City
NY 11101

> Electric foot pedal operated
> saddle staplers and similar gear.

The Type Aids Co.
238 Merrydale Rd.
San Rafael CA 94903

> Special purpose tools for design
> and production, including inch-pica
> conversion rulers, line gages, photo
> scalers, tracing paper with non-
> photographic grid.

> Publications that can direct you to
> printing supplies include:

COSMEP (Committee of Small Magazine Editors
and Publishers) *Newsletter*
PO Box 703
San Francisco CA 94101

Chartpak Catalog
Chartpak
1 River Rd.
Leeds MA 01053

> I use and like Chartpak presstype
> lettering; the catalog is free and
> instructive in many ways.

Fototype Catalog
Fototype, Inc.
1414 Roscoe St.
Chicago IL 60657

> The catalog, free on request, is full
> of information on setting heads as well
> as on other useful supplies.

Printer's Bargain News
Turnbaugh Printers Supply Co.
104 Sporting Hill Rd.
Mechanicsburg PA 17055

> Paper, other equipment in the machinery
> line, such as saddle staplers, small
> presses; a good source of information
> on such items available all over the
> U.S.

Swap or Buy: America's Leading National Publica-
tion of Graphic Arts Listings
343 Johnson Ave.
Brooklyn NY 11206

> Bimonthly; variety of ads for new
> and used printing equipment; free
> sample copy on request.

Appendix 6: Reviews, Sales

Pre-publication:

Set the publication date far enough in advance to send galley proofs or review copies to these media:

Kirkus Reviews
60 W. 13th St.
New York 10011

Kirkus goes primarily to librarians; in 1977 it reviewed 2,867 adult books and a total of 4,117 books; try to be realistic in assessing whether your book might be reviewed, and whether it has appeal to librarians.

Library Journal
1180 Ave. of the Americas
New York 10036

Part of the massive Bowker publications network; a review in this journal could be important to library sales.

Forecast
Baker & Taylor
1515 Broadway
New York 10036

If you plan to distribute the book nationally through bookstores, this

publication, by one of the major
booksellers, is important.

New York Times
Editor, Sunday Book Review Section
229 W. 43rd St
New York 10036

Reviewed 1,476 adult books in 1976,
2,255 in 1977, and a total of 2,622
books in 1977; can yours make the
grade?

"Weekly Record"
Publishers' Weekly
1180 Ave. of the Americas
New York 10036

Ask for an Advance Book Information
(ABI) form as soon as you know the
specs; send galleys as much in advance of the publication date as
possible, with price and date of
availability noted. If accepted,
the book will be listed the week
it is published, and automatically
listed in the *American Book Publishing Record.*

Free Listings:

Alternatives in Print: A Catalog of Social Change Publications
Glide Publications
330 Ellis St.
San Francisco CA 94102

> A catalog of publications "alternative" to mass-market material; write for information, as the catalog is widely distributed with the aid of grants.

Book Publishers Directory
Gale Research Co.
Book Tower
Detroit MI 48226

> Gale publishes *Contemporary Authors* and a wide variety of other materials with free listings; write for more information.

Committee of Small Magazine Editors and Publishers (COSMEP) *Newsletter*
Box 703
San Francisco CA 94101

> Features a regular section on new magazines, often announces book publications, gives information on various aspects of publishing; an extremely useful publication to anyone who is writing/publishing, and free to members of COSMEP; for more information, write, enclosing an SASE, and see Appendix 7.

Cumulative Book Index
H.W. Wilson Co.
950 University Ave.
New York 10452

> Ask for an information slip and return
> it with a copy of the book or a news
> release or other descriptive material;
> the *Index* is published monthly, with
> cumulations throughout the year and
> every two years; it lists all books
> printed in English and is distributed
> to about 10,000 bookstores and lib-
> raries; ask for a catalog listing other
> reference guides published by Wilson,
> most of which offer free or low-cost
> listing.

Daily Book Page
New York Times
229 W. 43rd St.
New York 10036

> This listing is selective; it does not
> include technical books, ones that are
> extremely specialized, textbooks, ju-
> venile books or doctoral theses. Send
> the book, with price information; the
> *Times* has a circulation of about
> 1,500,000. Do not try to economize by
> combining this mailing with a copy to
> the Sunday section mentioned earlier.

Small Press Record of Books
Dustbooks
Box 1056
Paradise CA 95969

The *Record* is annual, listing books
published by small presses and self-
publishing authors; each item is
indexed by author, title, publisher
and price; send a copy of the book
and descriptive material. Advertising
space is also available, at a lower
rate than for any publication mentioned so far. The same publisher
lists small press books monthly in
the *Small Press Review*, with a circulation of about 4,000; each issue
also carries reviews--you might submit the book for review, or include
a review with the copy you send, to
the address above; this listing
is not automatic either, but the
editors give careful attention to
all forms of self-publishing.

Other Review Sources:

Remember, even reviewers with special
interest in small presses are swamped
with material; reviewers for major
national publications are even busier.
Be reasonable in submitting your book--
does it really deserve or need national
publicity? Is a reviewer likely to select your book from hundreds of others?

I'm not trying to discourage you, but
to encourage realism in your choices of
reviewers to approach. It is difficult,
for example, to draw attention to poetry,
simply because it is never a big seller
for the major presses, and hence seldom published. As a result, a great deal
is published by small presses, and reviewers are deluged with it. If you con-
clude that national publicity is un-
likely, put your money into local promotion.

Booklist
American Library Association
50 E. Huron St.
Chicago Il 60611

Besides its regular reviews, this publication now also has a small press
section; free sample on request. Even
a short review in *Booklist* has brought
me many orders from librarians--for a
saddle-stitched poetry book! In 1977
Booklist reviewed 6,790 books.

Choice
Association of College and Research Libraries
American Library Association
100 Riverview Center
Middletown CT 06357

> With *Booklist* and *Library Journal*, this
> publication reaches and influences a lot
> of librarians. Send a review copy, and
> if the book isn't reviewed, send them
> a reminder in a month or two.

Editor and Publisher International Year Book
Editor and Publisher Co.
850 3rd Ave.
New York 10022

> This newspaper directory names de-
> partment heads and gives various
> information about each paper that
> might assist you in getting a review
> written or accepted.

Horn Book Magazine
585 Boylston St.
Boston MA 02116

> Specializes in children's books; a re-
> view here could be important, since
> the magazine goes to teachers as well
> as librarians.

Bill Katz
School of Library Science
State University of New York (SUNY)
1400 Washington Ave.
Albany NY 12203

>Publishes a regular column read by
>librarians, but when I wrote in 1976,
>he said to contact him again in 1979.

Library Journal
School Library Journal
R.R. Bowker Co.
1180 Ave. of the Americas
New York 10036

>Both publications are devoting more
>attention to small press publications
>in recent years.

Daniel Lusk
"Off the Wall"
PO Box 1038
Doylestown PA 18901

>Lusk's grant-financed radio review
>program treats small-press publications
>for national public radio stations, and
>is heard all over the country; send work
>for consideration. Lusk, a poet, is a
>knowledgeable reviewer.

The Pushcart Prize: Best of the Small Presses
Bill Henderson, ed.
Pushcart Press
Box 845
Yonkers NY 10701

Published annually, this fat collection
samples work of all kinds from independent publishers; send your work for
consideration, and include a request
for the book for some delightful and
sometimes surprising reading.

San Francisco Review of Books
2140 Vallejo St.
San Francisco CA 94123

Mostly West Coast publications.

Serials Librarian
Haworth Press
149 5th Ave.
New York 10010

A quarterly publication for librarians,
which accepts small magazines for
review; send a copy with press release
to Senior Bibliographer.

Small Press Review
Dustbooks
PO Box 1056
Paradise CA 95969

A monthly publication that reviews
dozens of books very thoroughly; Sub-
scribe at $10/year.

A variety of book review syndicates,
independent reviewers and similar
sources of potential reviews are
listed in the following sources.

282

The sources, most of them expensive, should be available in your library or through interlibrary loan. Search them for reviewers, for publications in your region that might review your book, or print news releases or your review of it. Also remember that radio or TV stations near you might use a news story or interview with the author, publisher or both.

Keep in mind that, contrary to what you may read, sending the reviewer information on the book with the suggestion that he send for a review copy will seldom bring results. Even the most indepent reviewer is bombarded with free books; he doesn't have time to write for review copies. So select the ones you think will give attention to your book, and send a copy, along with sufficient background information.

Request two copies of any review that they may write, and include an SASE to help insure that you get them.

Literary Market Place

Ulrich's International Periodicals Directory

Ayer Directory of Publications

Standard Periodical Directory

An Advertiser's Guide to Scholarly Periodicals
American University Press Services, Inc.
1 Park Ave.
New York 10016

> Updated periodically, this is valuable
> in finding specialized magazines for de-
> veloping lists of reviewers or mailing
> lists in specific academic areas.

Broadcasting Yearbook
Broadcasting Publications, Inc.
1735 DeSales St. NW
Washington DC 20036

> Directory to radio and TV stations and
> personnel, nationwide.

International Yearbook
Editor & Publisher
850 3rd Ave.
New York 10022

> An annual, comprehensive listing of
> newspapers nationally and their key
> personnel.

Syndicated Columnists
Richard Weiner
Richard Weiner, Inc.
888 7th Ave.
New York 10019

> Consider sending your book to some of
> these if it might have special reason
> to interest them.

Review Services:

These companies charge for their services; write for information and read any agreements carefully. Also ask for samples of reviews. I have written all three of the firms listed several times, enclosing my booklist and requesting information; I received no answer. I suspect that books with a commercial aspect might get more attention. And I wonder if editors of most publications would regard reviews from these companies seriously.

Book Preview
317 W. 89th St.
New York 10024

>   Report and review of book is printed in pamphlet sent to 2,021 bookstores and 25 national book clubs.

Superior Book Reviews
PO Drawer 32
San Angelo TX 76901

>   Book review and third party recommendation of book are printed and sent to 8500 booksellers.

Irwin Zucker
6565 Sunset Blvd.
Hollywood CA 90028

>   A monthly bulletin of book news and promotion.

Low-cost Advertising:

This is a short category because I've eliminated all sources of advertising that I feel would be out of reach of most small press publishers; many of these are listed in *LMP* if you want to check on them. I'm also convinced that, as discussed in the Glossary entry on promotion, other forms of publicity are more successful in encouraging sales for the small publisher.

R.R. Bowker
1180 Ave. of the Americas
New York 10036

Bowker's services are practically free; the company publishes a variety of guides to books which list publications at very low rates. These include *Books in Print, Publishers' Trade List Annual, Subject Guide to Books* and *Ulrich's International Periodicals Directory*, which go to more than 11,000 wholesalers, bookstores and libraries. Write for rates, submitting the following information: title of book, author's name, year of publication or expected publication, date, type and number of illustrations, number of pages, type of binding, price, specific subject of book (send a copy of contents page) and name and address where books may be purchased.

EBSCO Subscription Services
17-19 Washington Ave.
Tenafly NJ 07670

> Strictly for periodicals, this service
> publishes a *Librarians' Handbook*, listing
> 115,000 titles and sent to 20,000 libra-
> rians. Write for information. One of the
> publications of *The Huenefeld Report*
> (Appendix 9) says this kind of listing
> does no good, but you'll have to make
> your own judgment.

Distributors:

These distributors deal primarily in
small press books; send descriptive
information and a sample copy, along
with price and discount information;
include an SASE and postage for the
book if you want it returned.

B. DeBoer
188 High St.
Nutley NJ 07110

Distributes many little magazines, but
is not interested in books.

Bellows Distribution
919 16th Ave. NE
Rochester MN 55901

Various projects are underway to aid
small presses/publishers. For current
information, write the following:

Book People
2940 Seventh Ave.
Berkeley CA 94710

Bookslinger
PO Box 1625
2163 Ford Parkway
St. Paul MN 55116

CCLM (Coordinating Council of Literary Magazines)
80 Eighth Ave.
New York 10011

>   Has sponsored many distribution projects
>   for magazines; write.

COSMEP (Committee of Small Magazine Editors
and Publishers)
PO Box 703
San Francisco CA 94101

>   Ask about the COSMEP van, which carries
>   members' books all over the country for
>   promotion and sale, and about other
>   projects.

the distributors
702 S. Michigan
South Bend IN 46618

Ingram Books
347 Redwood Dr.
Nashville TN 37217

L-S Distributors
1161 Post St.
San Francisco CA 94109

Plains Distribution Service
PO Box 3112
Fargo ND 58102

Small Press Book Club
PO Box 100
Paradise CA 95969

Small Press Traffic
3841-B 24th St.
San Francisco CA 94114

Women in Distribution
PO Box 8858
Washington DC 20003

> Also refer to listings in "Publishers'
> Distributors and Sales Representatives"
> in *Literary Market Place;* these are
> categorized by territory and sometimes
> by interests, and some representatives
> might be willing to handle your books
> in their normal territories.

Jobbers:

Generally, the small publisher's best chance at steady sales lies with the jobber; bookstores take too high a discount and pay too slowly; distributors take larger discounts. Jobbers, giant wholesalers which sell to stores and libraries, usually take 20-25% discount or less, since they order in large quantities, pay in 60 days , and keep accurate, up-to-date records. Write for information; also contact Dustbooks (PO Box 1056, Paradise CA 95969) for current information on these businesses, and for additional lists. *Impact Magazine*, PO Box 61297, Sunnyvale, CA 94088, has a free credit service for small presses; send SASE for a list of bad accounts--bookstores or jobbers that don't pay promptly.

Academic Library Service
141 NE 38th Terr.
Oklahoma City OK 73105

Alesco
Box 1488
Madison WI 53701

Baker & Taylor
1515 Broadway
New York 10036

Ask for the address of the division closest to your area, and of those in other divisions if your book has national appeal.

Ballen Booksellers Int.
667 Austin Blvd.
Commack, LI,
NY 11725

Banta, RE, Bookseller
Crawfordsville IN 47933

Blackwell North America
1003 Fries Mill Rd.,
Blackwood NJ 08012

Blackwell North America
PO Box 2770
Portland OR 97208

Bookazine Co., Inc
303 W. 10th St.
New York 10014

Bro-Dart Books
500 Arch St.
Williamsport PA 17701

Charles W. Clark Co., Inc.
564 Smith St.
Farmingdale NY 11735

Dayton Hudson Booksellers
9340 James Ave. S.
Minneapolis MN 55431

Eastern Book Co.
131 Middle St.
Portland ME 04112

Emery-Pratt Co.
1966 W. Main St.
Owosso MI 48867

Grayson Book Service Inc.
138 S. Van Brunt St.
Englewood NJ 07631

Midwest Library Service
11400 Dorsett Rd.
Maryland Heights MO 63043

See also "Wholesalers" in *Literary Market Place*, noting the subdivisions of "Wholesalers in Special Subjects", "to Book Stores" and " to Schools and Libraries".

Bookstores:

Listed below are five of the largest
chain bookstores in the nation; they do
buy books from small publishers, but
they demand a professional attitude
about filling orders, and often require a large number of copies. Direct
your inquiry to "Book Buyer".

Doubleday Book Shops
673 5th Ave.
New York 10022

Dayton-Hudson
9340 James Ave. S.
Minneapolis MN 55431

Cokesbury
201 8th Ave. S.
Nashville TN 37203

Walden Book Company
179 Ludlow St.
Stamford CT 06904

Brentano's
6 W. 48 St.
New York 10017

Other booksellers may be located in
these sources:

Literary Market Place

The American Book Trade Directory

> A Bowker publication, this is biennial,
> with lists of more than 17,500 book-
> sellers, publishers and wholesalers
> in the U.S. and Canada, arranged by
> city and state and annotated; try
> the library.

Directory of College Stores
B. Klein Publications
Box 8503
Coral Springs FL 33065

> Annotated; you might find a copy at
> a university bookstore.

American Odyssey: A Bookselling Travelogue
by Len Fulton with Ellen Ferber
(Dustbooks, PO Box 1056, Paradise, CA 95969)

> Lists dozens of bookstores all over
> the nation, with Fulton's personal
> annotations, result of his visits
> while selling some of his publications.
> Check it for bookstores in your area,
> and for those receptive to small
> press work in other areas.

Exhibits, Book Fairs

Many companies stage book exhibits, with representatives of academic institutions, libraries and other markets invited. I've never been able to trace many orders directly to such exhibits, but they do furnish a way of getting information brochures in the hands of customers, particularly librarians, who may order later. However, some exhibit services' fees are prohibitive. Write for information. Also watch COSMEP *Newsletter* for smaller exhibits sponsored by small press organizations.

American Bookseller Association
800 2nd Ave.
New York 10017

The *Huenefeld Report* indicates small publishers have a better chance at ABA exhibits than at larger ones dominated by major publishers.

Book Mail Service, Inc.
82-27 164 St.
Jamaica NY 11432

Deals in paperbound books.

Books On Exhibit
Mount Kisco NY 10549

Exhibits of library and professional books for schools and other institutions.

College Marketing Group, Inc.
198 Ash St.
Reading MA 01867

>Displays books and related materials through mobile display units at more than 300 colleges and universities around the country.

The Combined Book Exhibit, Inc.
Westchester Publishing Park
Ossining NY 10562

>Arranges more than 125 exhibits for schools, libraries, professional and scholarly meetings.

Educational Reading Service Book Fairs, Inc.
320 Route 17
Mahwah NJ 07430

The New England Mobile Book Fair, Inc.
82 Needham St.
Newton Highlands, MA 02161

>Exhibits juvenile books, new books, classics; sponsoring group receives percentage of sales.

Mary Griffin Newton
16525 Plainview
Detroit MI 48219

>Exhibits for book clubs, churches, libraries, schools; both adult and juvenile books.

Periodical Exposition Displays
235 Park Ave. S.
New York 10003

> Periodicals and books exhibited to
> librarians and others.

Schanharr-Gottstein
PO Box 558
Corte Madera CA 94925

> Exhibits small press titles at in-
> ternational book fairs, and at library
> and booksellers' conventions.

> For more possibilities, consult:

Directory of Exhibit Opportunities
The Association of American Publishers
1 Park Ave.
New York 10016

> An annotated, chronological listing
> of more than 600 exhibits nationwide;
> check interlibrary loan or a larger
> publisher for a copy.

Literary Market Place

Appendix 7:

Mailing Lists, Services

The organizations listed in this
section supply readymade mailing
lists, printed on labels to be
applied to the mailing piece that
you supply.

Before you order, find out if the
list is rented for one-time use only;
this is most often the case. Also,
ask about the kind of labels; self-
adhesive labels can be peeled from
the backing sheet and applied quickly
to the mailing piece, while the
"lick-and-stick" variety must be
moistened and applied. The latter
referred to by most as gummed labels,
tend to blur, often are not as easy
to apply evenly and sometimes come
off in postal sorting machines.
"Cheshire labels" are $3\frac{1}{2}''$ by 13/16",
and intended for machine application.

The first four sources of lists
have been most often recommended by
small press publishers; the rest
are in random order since I have
no personal experience with them.

COSMEP Mailing Service
Lee Laughlin
PO Box 29214, Presidio
San Francisco CA 94129

These lists are simply the best that
a small publisher can obtain, since
COSMEP began compiling lists of
bookstores and libraries in 1969
and offers prices lower than those
of commercial mailing list companies, even on small orders. Lists
of 2900 libraries and 3900 bookstores
are available for rental on self-
adhesive labels at $30 for the first
thousand, with a 10% discount on
every thousand after that. So if
you order 2,000 labels, the price is
$57; 3,000 are $82.50 and so on. A
list of 1055 college and university
libraries rents for a flat fee of $35.
Orders must be paid for in advance,
or they will be shipped C.O.D., a
practice which reduces overhead. On
prepaid orders, Service pays postage
and handling; on C.O.D. orders the
buyer pays. Minimum order is 1,000
labels, shipped by third class mail
unless the buyer requests otherwise,
in which case add $1.50 for airmail
postage.

The only breakdown possible is by
states. You may contact Service for
the number of names in any given
state or states. You may also rent
the COSMEP membership list if you join
the organization.

300

Education Mailings Clearing House
Roxbury Bldg.
Sweet Springs MO 65351

> I rank this one second because of its
> "incredibly low prices" as the COSMEP
> *Newsletter* states. Ask for a catalog
> and price list; lists include schools,
> libraries and institutions. Basic
> charge, which includes list rental and
> addressing (either you ship the item
> to be mailed to them, or send the en-
> velopes, which they'll return addressed)
> is $7.65 per thousand. They offer
> additional services, such as mailing
> to selected zip codes, or altering
> addresses so the mailing piece reaches
> a particular officer in the institution
> addressed. A number of other services
> are described in the free catalog.

Resources
Box 314, Harvard Square
Cambridge MA 12138

> Offers a sample list of 1-300 names
> from any of its lists for $3-$9; fast
> service, inexpensive prices. Example:
> 3000 colleges and universities for
> $60. Varied subjects; write for infor-
> mation.

R.R. Bowker
Mailing List Division
1180 Ave. of the Americas
New York 10036

> Bowker has been in the book informa-
> tion business for more than a century,

and has voluminous, well-developed
lists of almost everyone, divided into
small categories. For example, you can
order a list of 1,190 public libraries
with book funds over $25,000 for $30,
or one of 290 Catholic libraries for
$20, or a list of 2,695 Environmenta-
lists for $100. You pay more than for
some other lists, but you get extremely
specific lists, which may be just what
you need. Bowker reserves the right to
request a sample mailing piece or pro-
posed copy before agreeing to release
its lists. First orders require pre-
payment and are for one-time use only.
Bowker also has a higher fee for mailing
your promotional piece for you.

American Library Association
50 E. Huron St.
Chicago IL 60611

College Marketing Group, Inc.
198 Ash St.
Reading MA 01867

> Lists of college professors, available
> by discipline or courses taught.

Dependable Lists, Inc.
257 Park Ave. S.
New York 10010

> For $1 supplies a useful *Selected Guide
> to List Markets* which specifies 25,000
> detailed lists available; Sample: 213,000
> women executives at $25M; 4,500 children's
> camps at $25M.

Alan Drey Co.
333 N. Michigan Ave.
Chicago IL 60601

> This is a mailing list broker, who
> reportedly can get any list you want;
> inquire about prices.

Dunn & Bradstreet
50 Bridge St.
Manchester NH 03101

Dunhill International List Co.
444 Park Ave. S.
New York 10016

> Compiles lists of domestic corporations
> and individuals by occupations; 44-page
> descriptive catalog free on request.
> Sample entry: "26,000 Earthworm buyers--
> $30 Buyers of earthworm breeding stock
> and earthworm books. . .list includes
> both men and women who desire to estab-
> lish their own bait business, as well as
> fishermen and gardeners. Average sale
> $40. 1975-77." If there's an entry that
> suits your book, this could be an ex-
> tremely useful list because you can cal-
> culate how much the addressees might
> pay for the information you supply.

The Educational Directory
126 Blaine Ave.
Marion OH 43302

> Lists of college faculties and libraries,
> available by field of interest or geo-
> graphically.

Market Data Retrieval
800 Boston Post Rd.
Westport CT 06880

    Educational mailing lists that seem to
be quite specialized; you can, for
example, select faculty members teaching
linguistics, paying $30 per 1,000.

Peterson's Guides
Distribution Service
228 Alexander St.
Princeton NJ 08540

    College and university lists, including
administrators and heads of academic
divisions; Peterson's provides various
services; write for free information.

Response Mailing Lists
39 Pine Dr.
Park Ridge NJ 07656

    Computerized mailing lists; more than
12,000.

School Lists Mailing Corp.
1710 Highway 35
Oakhurst NJ 07755

    Detailed selection of lists by subject
matter and age level of elementary
and secondary school teachers; also
categories of audio-visual, remedial
reading and administrative; in addition
lists the less than 1/10 of 1% of
personnel who supervise curriculum
planning, if you have a text book to
market.

304

Writer's Digest
9933 Alliance Rd.
Cincinnati OH 45242

List of 250,000 buyers of books, courses
and magazines for writers; write for
information.

Also refer to *Literary Market Place* for
additional suppliers of mailing lists.

Sources:

Even if you use lists provided by other services, you might still have a number of ways to continue development of your own lists. First, keep a record of the name and address of everyone who orders a book from you. Type names and addresses on mailing labels, possibly grouped by zip code or according to whether the names are of institutions, individuals, businesses, booksellers or the like.

You may also develop lists by using some of the sources listed below. And if your work focuses on a very specific subject, such as trimming the hooves on a rodeo horse, look for the organization likely to be interested in the subject--such as the Rodeo Cowboys' Association. Once you've located such a group (use the lists of organizations in the library) write and ask if you can use their membership list, explaining your purpose and perhaps enclosing a copy of the book. If officials like it, you might even get additional promotion in the organization newsletter.

An Advertiser's Guide to Scholarly Periodicals
American University Press Services, Inc.
1 Park Ave.
New York 10016

Updated periodically; valuable in finding specialized magazines directed to specific academic interests.

American Book Trade Directory

> Published by Bowker, this contains a
> comprehensive listing of bookstores,
> wholesalers and other book outlets
> in the U.S. and Canada.

American Library Directory

> Also by Bowker, this biennial book
> lists libraries and library schools
> in the U.S., Canada, overseas.

Membership Directory
American Library Association

> An annual listing of libraries in
> the ALA; check your library.

Direct Mail List Rates and Data
Business Publication Rates and Data
Standard Rate and Data Service, Inc.
5201 Old Orchard Rd.
Skokie IL 60076

> Publications by this organization,
> which also supplies mailing lists.

Encyclopedia of Associations
Gale Research Co.
Book Tower
Detroit MI 48226

National Radio Publicity Directory
Peter Glenn Publications Ltd.
17 E. 48 St.
New York 10017

> Lists and describes 2500 radio talk
> shows, nationally.

National Research Bureau, Inc.
424 N. 3rd St.
Burlington IA 52601

> Publishes listings of newspapers, maga-
> zines, tv and radio stations, feature
> writers, photographers and syndicates,
> and internal publications. Write for
> information and costs.

*National Trade and Professional Associations
of the U.S. and Canada and Labor Unions*
Columbia Books, Inc.
Suite 601, 734 15 St. N.W.
Washington DC 20005

> This annual indexes 6000 associations
> and labor unions by location and pro-
> fession.

"Selected Guide to List Markets"
Dependable Lists, Inc.
257 Park Ave. S.
New York 10010

> Besides showing you Dependable Lists'
> wares, this publication has a lot of
> information on mailing lists in general.
> The cover says the price is $1, but I
> wrote on company stationery and got
> the catalog without charge.

Mailing Services:

These companies sort, bundle and mail
your promotional pieces; rates are
generally low. In the San Francisco
area, talk to:

Lee Laughlin
COSMEP Mailing Service
PO Box 29214, Presidio
San Francisco CA 94129

about mailing services; in other metropolitan areas, look in the yellow pages
of the telephone directory under "letter
shop services," or "publishers' shipping
services".

Accurate Mail/Marketing Corp.
32-02 Queens Blvd.
Long Island City
New York 11101

Boffer Corp.
111 8th Ave.
New York 10011

Direct Mail Promotions
342 Madison Ave.
New York 10017

Will include your promotional material
in a bulletin mailed to a regular list
of their own, as well as sending your
material by itself to a list you sel-
lect; for example, you may mail one

of your own pieces, 8½ x 11, to 6,000
public libraries for $350. I find some
of their promotional pieces garish; you
might want to have control over items
mailed with yours.

Distribution Systems, Inc.
460 Howell St.
Bristol PA 19007

Excell Mail & Book Service
235-41 W. 1st St.
Bayonne NY 07002

Gropper Packaging Co.
25 Washington St.
Brooklyn NY 11201

Prices are based on the size of books,
and the number shipped, and they handle
orders from firms that sell as few as
1-2 titles, 5-6 books per month. Sample
price: 15¢/jiffy bag; 59¢ postage (after
July 1979); handling charge 17¢/book for
a total of 91¢/book.

Publishers Warehouse Inc.
7 Bushwick Pl.
Brooklyn NY 11206

Also consult *Literary Market Place* for
additional listings; I wrote twice to
the following without receiving a reply:
J.V. Corporation, Publishers Service,
Quarto Book Service, T.E. Enterprises,
W.A. Book Service.

Appendix 8:

Writers' Organizations

Write to appropriate organizations for
information on their benefits and publications, which often include tax and publishing tips. Professional status is
sometimes enhanced by membership in these
organizations.

Academy of American Poets
1078 Madison Ave.
New York 10028

American Society of Writers
PO Box 488
Lake Placid NY 12946

The Authors League of America, Inc.
234 44 St.
New York 10036

A national membership corporation, to
promote interests of authors and play-
wrights, work for copyright legislation,
guard freedom of expression.

COSMEP (Committee of Small Magazine
Editors and Publishers
PO Box 703
San Francisco CA 94101

You need not already be publishing to
join this group, and the monthly newsletter is packed with information on
every phase of publishing, writing,
distribution; certainly one of the
first organizations you should join if
you are serious about publishing your
work in any way.

CCLM (Coordinating Council of Literary Magazines)
80 Eighth Ave.
New York 10011

A national nonprofit organization
which sponsors aid programs to
noncommercial literary magazines,
for continued publication and for
authors' payments; write for information on this and other functions of
CCLM.

National Institute of Arts and Letters
633 W. 155 St.
New York 10032

National League of American Pen Women, Inc.
1300 17th St. NW
Washington DC 10036

National Writers Club, Inc.
1365 Logan St.
Denver CO 80203

A nonprofit representative organization
of new and established writers.

P.E.N. American Center
156 5th Ave.
New York 10010

An international organization of writers
which sponsors various publications,
especially on grants to writers.

The Poetry Society of America
National Arts Club
15 Gramercy Park
New York 10003

Poets and Writers
201 W. 54 St.
New York 10019

Publishes many useful pamphlets and
books available to members and non-
members; unlike some groups which ask
only dues, Poets and Writers requires
a certain number of publications.

Women in Communications, Inc.
National Headquarters
8305-A School Creek Blvd.
Austin TX 78758

Both *Literary Market Place* and *Writer's
Market,* as well as various writers' magazines, list dozens more writer's clubs
and conferences in various states, as
well as national organizations. Clubs
are generally more informal and social.
Many very special interest groups exist,
such as the Construction Writers Assoc.,
the Mystery Writers, and even the Dog
Writers' Assoc.

Appendix 9:

Bibliography
General Sources:

American Odyssey: A Bookselling Travelogue
by Len Fulton with Ellen Ferber
187 pp., 1975, $4.50 paper, $7.95 cloth
Dustbooks
PO Box 1056
Paradise CA 95969

Len and Ellen's story of how they
loaded the car with copies of his
novel and traveled from the West
Coast to the East visiting book
stores in an experiment in personal
promotion; delightful reading as en-
tertainment, as well as being filled
with information on stores, annotated
with comments on how the itinerant
novelist was received; also lists
stores in the back.

Ayer Directory of Publications

Published annually since 1869, this
is a directory of print media including
daily and weekly newspapers and magazines
(consumer, business, technical, trade
and farm) with information on finances,
trade area, circulation; helpful in
sending news releases, ads, planning
news stories.

314

"A Book's Calendar"
Charles A. Aronson
Writer Publisher
RR 1, Hundred Acres
Arcade NY 14009

> Reprinted from Aronson's book *The Writer Publisher,* the calendar includes the Advance Book Information form for Bowker and--most useful--a checklist of steps to be followed in publishing and promoting your book. Aronson is bitter about his encounters with subsidy publishers, and his book is educational on that score, but poorly reproduced and concentrates heavily on hardsell promotion.

Books: From Writer to Reader
Howard Greenfeld
(New York: Crown, 1976)

> A nontechnical step-by-step description; good introduction to the processes of printing.

Books and Printing: A Treasury for Typophiles
Paul A. Bennett, ed.,
(New York: World, 1951)

> Delightful essays by people who love their work; don't try to read this as preparation for becoming a publisher, but save it for late some winter night when you have a bottle of good wine and your books have been delayed by a teamster strike.

*Bookmaking: The Illustrated Guide to Design
and Production*
Marshall Lee
(New York: Bowker, 1965)

> This has the most information on all
> phases of printing I've found in any
> single book; much of it is relatively
> useless to the small printer, practi-
> cally speaking, because the book is
> written to explain the big commercial
> publishing house operation. Still, for
> details and background information on
> every technical phase of book produc-
> tion--from design through promotion--
> consult this book. Its orientation is
> also to "having" things done rather
> than doing them yourself, but Lee's
> explanations of operations are clear
> and straightforward and it is copiously
> illustrated.

The Bookman's Glossary
(New York: Bowker)

> This guide to terminology includes both
> production phases and distribution to
> bookstores, libraries and collectors,
> but almost any term you don't find in
> *The Book Book* is in it; your library
> should have it.

*The Bowker Annual of Library and Book Trade
Information*
R.R. Bowker
1180 Ave. of the Americas
New York 10036

> Loaded with useful and educational in-
> formation: the number of libraries in

316

the U.S., their budgets, total number
of books published by category (agri-
culture, travel, history), sales figures, average prices of books, legislation of interest to the library
and book trade, lists of books useful to the library or book trade,
associations; all this can help you
plan mailing lists, organize promotion, or simply make you more know-
ledgeable about your chosen field.

Bowker catalog
R.R. Bowker
1180 Ave. of the Americas
New York 10036

Available free, the catalog is full
of information, and can help you develop
promotional ideas.

Commercial Artist Handbook
John Snyder
1973, hardbound, 264 pp., $10.95
(New York: Watson-Guptill)

Useful to small publishers because
of its emphasis on tools; unfortunately
he assumes the reader is an idiot in
some instances (with a drawing of a
razor blade, for example) but he also
includes many tips normally picked up
only after years of experience.

The Co-Op Publishing Handbook
Michael Scott Cain, ed.,
1978, 208 pp., $3.95 paper, $8.95 cloth
Dustbooks
PO Box 1056
Paradise CA 95969

Discusses vanity and self-publishing as
well as co-ops; articles from/about
a variety of cooperative publishers,
detailing how to and how not to, as
well as membership qualifications.
With Bill Henderson's *The Publish-It-
Yourself Handbook*, this is simply the
best, most concise source available for
understanding the principles and prac-
tices of self-publishing in any form.
Cain gives an excellent history of self-
publishing and a review of what's really
happening in the major publishing houses
today to encourage growth among smaller
publishers.

*Directory of Private Presses and
Letterpress Printers and Publishers*
1978, $5
Press of Arden Park
861 Los Molinos Way
Sacramento CA 95825

Check this source for two reasons: you
might find a press listed that would
publish your book at no cost to you, or
you can find printers who will submit
bids for publishing to your specifications. Most of the listings are for
letterpress printers, who are capable
books that are truly art objects in
themselves.

The Encyclopedia of Self-Publishing
Marylyn and Tom Ross
 Communication Creativity
1340 Tourmaline St.
San Diego CA 92109

Announced as "the most comprehensive
manual ever produced" on self-publishing,
this book appears to cover the subject
pretty well, judging from the contents
preview I received. Some phrases, such as
"choosing a marketable subject and title",
and "how to get a free nationwide author
tour" lead me to believe the text is
oriented toward books with some solid
commercial appeal, rather than poetry,
fiction and the like. However, it looks
like a good source; I have not seen it,
because the price--$29.95--is prohibitive.

Fototype Catalog
Fototype, Inc.
1414 Roscoe St.
Chicago IL 60657

The free catalog is one place you may
study and compare type faces, as it
gives examples of common ones. Fototype
is different from presstype in that
letters are arranged on white paper,
so spacing is done for you. I think
it's more difficult to handle, but
the company has attractive introduc-
tory offers if you're setting up to
do more than one book; the catalog
is worthwhile for the information
alone.

Graphics Handbook
Ken Garland
(New York: Reinhold Publishing Corp., 1966)

Veddy veddy British, but has useful
sections on tools, folding and binding,
and concepts in graphic arts

How to Publish Your Own Book
L.W. Mueller
paper, $4.95
Harlo Press
16721 Hamilton Ave.
Detroit MI 48203

> Harlo is a subsidy publisher and Mueller
> its president, so the orientation is
> clear; however, he gives useful in-
> formation on preparing a manuscript
> for publication, as well as extensive
> advice on self-promotion; written in
> terms a novice can understand and
> with practical illustrations.

How to Get Happily Published
Judith Appelbaum and Nancy Evans
1978, 272 pp.
(Harper & Row)

> Excellent on why to self-publish, with
> lots of comforting examples; also good
> on sources of all kinds of information
> relative to writing and publishing; bulk
> of book is how to write a manuscript and
> increase its chances of being accepted
> by editors, rather than self-publishing;
> cheery but knowledgeable style.

How to Publish, Promote and Sell Your
Book: A Guide for the Self-Publishing Author
Joseph V. Goodman
Adams Press
30 W. Washington St.
Chicago IL 60602

> Goodman runs Adams press, a subsidy
> house; extremely commercial in orienta-
> tion, but with some useful sections,
> notably on income tax and the hazards

320

of vanity publishing; most of his extensive reference lists are from
Literary Market Place and some information is outdated or downright wrong.

The Huenefeld Report
PO Box U
Bedford MA 01730

Billed as a report for managers and
and planners in "modest-sized book
publishing houses", the report is
not really intended for small press
publishers; yearly rate is $48 for
26 issues. But they offer individual
reports at reasonable rates, and the
reports are well-written. Ask for a
list and select the ones you need.
For example, I learned a lot from
"How Small Publishers Sell Their
Books to Bookstores", "Getting Your
Money Early: Pre-publication Promotion and Selling", "How to do Business
with Book Wholesalers", "How to Sell
More of Your Books to Libraries", and
"How to Make Mail Order Bookselling
Pay Off", all for $15.

Internal Revenue Service Publications
IRS
1111 Constitution Ave.
Washington DC 20224

IRS issues many good, clearly written
pamphlets to help writers and small
press publishers; ask for information
on tax breaks for small businesses,

self-employment, keeping records for
small businesses, and taxes for the
self-employed.

The International Directory of Little Maga-
zines and Small Presses
Dustbooks
PO Box 1056
Paradise CA 95969

Published since 1965, this is the one
reliable source to the world of the
small press, publishing books, magazines, broadsides, poemcards and many
other forms; more than 2500 presses
are represented in over 140 categories
of interest and all over the U.S. and
several other countries. Entries tell
much about the publication: editors'
names, type of material used, comments
by the editors, frequency of publication, prices, type of printing, discount schedules, membership in organizations, payment arrangements, rights
purchased. Indexes in the back divide
publications by interest and geogra-
phically, list distributors and explain
the acronyms of various organizations.

Literary Agents: A Complete Guide
Poets & Writers, Inc.
201 W. 54 St.
New York 10019

What agents are, what they do, how to
find one, names and addresses of some
selected agencies interested in li-

terary work and a chart illustrating
the rights involved in a sale; bibliography.

*Literary Market Place: Directory of American
Book Publishing*
R.R. Bowker
1180 Ave. of the Americas
New York 10036

Universally referred to as *LMP*; perhaps the single potentially most useful source for any publisher--but most
of us don't refer to it enough because
it's too expensive to buy annually and
even many libraries get it only every
2 or 3 years; contains information in
these categories: book publishing;
associations; book trade events;
courses, conferences and contests;
agents and agencies; services and
supplies; direct mail promotion; review, selection and reference; radio,
television and motion pictures; wholesale, export and import; book manufacturing; magazine and newspaper
publishing; names and numbers, with
dozens of more specific individual
categories that give you a clue to the
whereabouts of virtually any service
related to publishing that you need.
LMP's orientation is, of course, to
giant publishing companies, so in many
cases the companies listed may feel a
small or self-publisher's orders are
too small to deal with; however you
can learn a great deal about the entire industry by studying this source,

and reference to it will keep you from being tied to a single high-priced supplier of anything you need by enabling you to check with other suppliers everywhere in the nation.

Modern Graphic Arts Paste-Up: The Workshop Approach to the Graphic Arts
Gerald A. Silver
Graphic Arts Series
American Technical Society, 6608 Stony Island Ave. Chicago IL 60637

A source I wish I'd found when I began publishing; the workbook approach makes this a clear, practical text, with easy access to the information you need at any moment. The major drawback is the author's assumption that this is to be a classroom text, or that you are already familiar with the specialized language of graphic arts; there is, however, a good glossary, and a list at the end of each chapter of new words introduced. The emphasis is on the artistic aspect of layout, but if you're not capable of the detailed layout drawings Silver discusses, you can make do with rough sketches. Or wait until you have the actual elements of the pasteup and experiment with arrangements until you find the one you want. The workbook aspect allows you to practice on simulated projects. For example, you are taught how to use various types of transfer lettering, to recognize which type faces are most legible, to use white space as an

element of design, to use acetate film,
to order tint screens, design a display advertisement, scale photographs
and copy, crop pictures, paste up
pages using multiple colors, create
an imitation duotone. This is definitely one of the most useful sources
available.

Pocket Pal: A Graphic Arts Production Handbook
International Paper Co.
220 E. 42 St.
New York 10017

First produced in 1934, this small
(pocket size) book is loaded with information about graphic arts and
printing; much of it is oriented to
commercial publishing and thus more
complex than necessary for the first
time small publisher, but it has
more information in a smaller, more
accessible space than any other source.

Printing It
Clifford Burke
paper, 127 pp., 1972
(Berkeley: Wingbow Press; distributed by
Book People
2940 7th Ave.
Berkeley CA 94710

Filled with useful information in
readable terms, but oriented to the
reader who plans to set up a shop and
go into job printing as well as self-
publication.

*The Publish-It-Yourself Handbook: Literary
Tradition and How-To*
Bill Henderson, ed.
paper, 362 pp., 1973
The Pushcart Book Press
Box 845
Yonkers NY 10701

> In its 8th printing, this is a highly
> philosophical book, but the best source
> around for convincing yourself that
> self-publishing is better than waiting
> around for the big publishers to develop
> a taste for good writing. Henderson
> collects commentary from the famous and
> infamous self-publishers at various
> financial levels; many are especially
> inspirational since they discuss their
> work with an obvious love of the art of
> printing. In addition, the "Selected
> Manufacturers" section lists a number
> of volume printers specializing in
> short-run work, and the bibliography
> has sources for almost every phase of
> writing, publishing and promotion.

*Publish It Yourself: The Complete Guide to Self-
Publishing Your Own Book*
Charles J. Chickadel
paper, 1978, $5.95
Trinity Press
Box 1320
San Francisco CA 94101

> Chickadel is an experienced self-
> publisher, who self-published this book
> as a demonstration; lots of know-
> ledgeable commentary on various phases,
> but he plunges into discussion in
> terms that are never clearly defined;

somewhat vague on methods, such as
layout and pasteup.

The Shoestring Publisher's Guide
Nicholas Raeder and Regina B. Longyear
paper, 1974, 129 pp.
Sol III Publications
Box 751, One Wilson Rd.
Farmington ME 04938

Oriented toward magazine or periodical
publication and owning your own equipment; still this is good on most aspects
of doing it yourself; even includes
samples of common text and cover papers.

Small Press Record of Books in Print
Dustbooks
PO Box 1056
Paradise CA 95969

Lists approximately 7,500 books from
more than 1,000 presses, or around
80 to 90% of the titles produced by
small presses; indexed by author, by
title, publisher and subject. This
book is one way to locate publishers
who might cooperate in producing your
book.

*The Visual Artist's Guide to the New Copyright
Law*
Graphic Artists Guild
30 E. 20 St.
New York 10003

Essential for artists and useful for
anyone working with art, this source
explains the new copyright law that became effective Jan. 1, 1978; other

327

publications available from the same
source for visual artists include:
Legal Guide for the Visual Artist, and
Pricing and Ethical Guidelines; also
inquire about membership in the guild.

Writer's Market
9933 Alliance Rd.
Cincinnati OH 45242

Published annually, this marketing
directory for freelance writers lists
4,500 places to publish, with detailed
information about each; also designates
subsidy and royalty book publishers,
and supplies lots of general information;
in related areas, the company publishes
*Photographer's Market, Artist's Market,
Songwriter's Market* and *Craftworker's
Market,* all annuals; should be in the
library.

Bookbinding:

Basic Bookbinding
A.W. Lewis
(New York: Dover, 1957)

> This source covers basic binding and
> simple methods, progressing from
> binding of single and multi-sectioned
> books to case and library binding;
> sequences are reviewed in handy brief
> lists in the back, and, perhaps most
> helpful, Lewis discusses the differ-
> ences between English and U.S. terms
> and lists suppliers of materials.

Bookbinding for Beginners
John Corderoy
(New York: Watson-Guptill, 1967)

> Too complex for beginners; too many
> tools are required; lists other sources
> but many are from England.

Creative Bookbinding
Pauline Johnson
(Seattle: University of Washington Press, 1963)

> Though this book approaches bookbinding
> as an art form, it is the best source
> I've found for the beginner; it begins
> with clear, step-by-step drawings and
> instructions about simple processes:
> binding expanding files, folders, desk
> blotters, note pads, scrapbooks, port-
> folios, box files. Then it moves on to

more complex projects, with instructions
complemeted by photos and drawings. In
addition, the book opens with a fas-
cinating history of books, writing and
binding, and an excellent section on
design.

Introduction to Book Binding
Lionel S. Darley
(London: Faber & Faber, 1965)

A very English book, with differing
terms, English prices and a professional
manner, with strict requirements in
equipment and time. Begins with simple
jobs and moves toward more complex ones;
good glossary and bibliography, though
the latter lists mostly English sources.

Contests, Awards:

Hundreds of awards exist, many for work written or published on very specific topics, as well as more general awards in all types of literature for all age groups. See *Writer's Market*, *Literary Market Place*, and contact CCLM and COSMEP; in each source, check not only listings under awards and contests, but those listed for various writers' groups.

Awards, Honors and Prizes: A Directory and Source Book
Paul Wasserman, author and publisher
1963

A good general reference, indexed by subject and annotated.

Awards List
Poets & Writers, Inc.
201 W. 54 St.
New York 10019

100 grants, fellowships and prizes offered in the U.S. to poets and fiction writers; cross-indexed; free to writers listed with Poets & Writers.

CCLM (Coordinating Council of Literary Magazines)
80 Eighth Ave.
New York 10011

COSMEP (Committee of Small Press Editors and
Publishers)
PO Box 703
San Francisco CA 94101

Literary and Library Prizes
R.R. Bowker
1180 Ave. of the Americas
New York 10036

> Covers all major literary prizes, in-
> cluding fellowships to some writers
> conferences and those offered by
> the National Endowment for the Arts;
> find it in the library.

Pushcart Book Press
PO Box 845
Yonkers NY 10701

> Bill Henderson's Pushcart publishes an
> annual anthology of writing from small
> presses; submit your book or magazine
> selection for possible inclusion; and
> while you're at it, ask them to send
> you the next edition, with an invoice.

Courses:

Guide to Book Publishing Courses: Academic and Professional Programs
Peterson's Guides
228 Alexander St., Dept. F81
Princeton NJ 08540

> Details full-time and part-time programs in publishing offered in the U.S., including regular college and university courses, special academic institutes, seminars, workshops, internships at university presses, educational meetings of professional associations, and evening classes of trade organizations; with bibliography.

National University Extension Association
Suite 360, 1 Dupont Circle
Washington DC 20036

> Various continuing-education programs exist all over the U.S.; this organization publishes directories of correspondence and independent study courses, as well as on-campus programs; send for the free list of publications.

> *Literary Market Place* and *Writer's Market* list many colleges and universities offering courses in all phases of the book trade. Write the schools for additional information.

Design:

The Design of Books
Adrian Wilson
(London: Studio Vista, 1967)

> Oriented toward large operations,
> but loaded with good information,
> especially on design of various types
> of books, jackets and covers; also
> sections on the history and design
> of type, printing methods, the kinds,
> uses and sizes of paper, and binding.

Design with Type
Carl Dair
(University of Toronto Press, 1967)

> Excellent introduction to elements
> of type style; even flipping through
> it can give you a lesson in visual
> impact.

*Editing by Design: Word-and-Picture
Communication for Editors and Designers*
Jan V. White
(New York: Bowker, 1974)

> This book deals primarily with the
> problems confronting designers of
> magazine formats, and is estremely
> detailed, with lots of solid advice
> for someone working on a company
> publication, where you may be stuck
> with dull pictures. In addition, it's

the best source I've found for any
type of publishing design, with
examples of the effect of varied
column widths, type families and
their qualities, the effects of texture, tone, photo size, photo cap-
tions, graphs and charts, the use
of headlines, lists of sources of
inexpensive illustrations, and
the treatment of photographs to
vary the impression they give.
Whatever you plan to publish, try
to study a copy of this book.

Printing Types: An Introduction
Alexander Lawson
(Boston: Beacon Press)

Intended as a source for learning
to recognize and identify type, this
is useful for its multitude of examples and wealth of background information. You might want to study the
samples when determining the style
of your book.

See also the general section of App. 9;
if a source is good on design, I mention
that fact. A number of periodicals devoted to design and printing are listed in
Ulrich's. Ask for sample copies of these;
there will probably be a charge.

Print
R.C. Publications
355 Lexington Ave.
New York 10017

Design Magazine
1100 Waterway Blvd.
Indianapolis IN 46206

Graphics
Cody Publications, Inc.
Box 1030
Kissimmee FL 32741

Graphics Today
Syndicate Magazines
6 E. 43 St.
New York 10017

Grants:

Volumes could--and have--been written
on the whole subject of applying for and
getting grants. If you can finance your
own project instead of applying for a
grant, you will probably publish more
quickly. And you won't have to decide
whether government support of the arts
is legitimate.

But if you do apply for a grant, the
first problem is finding agencies with
funds that might be interested in the
project you are proposing. Two primary
methods exist: finding lists of organizations that give grants, and finding
lists of the grants they have previously
given. The existing sources, listed
below, give information mainly on
national foundations.

Also don't forget regional or state
companies that may have grant money
available without publicizing that
fact. I would advise checking listings
in the library for foundations in
your state or area, before you widen
your search to include national foundations, which are subject to many
more applications anyway.

Remember that more than 1,000 towns
and cities have local arts councils
that can provide grants to individuals
and organizations; check with your

local art center, chamber or commerce
or state arts council to locate the one
nearest you.

The Foundation Center
888 7th St.
New York 10019

> The greatest single source of grant
> information; can also direct you to
> regional information; the following
> publications are available from
> The Foundation Center, or may be
> obtained through your library.

Foundation Directory

> The most important reference work on
> foundations that make grants awards;
> lists 2800 large foundations (those
> with assets of more than a million
> dollars or grants exceeding $100,000
> annually); detailed information on
> each foundation including grants made;
> lists 90% of major foundations
> accounting for 80% of grants.

Foundation Center Source Book Profile

> Analytical profiles of more than
> 500 foundations per year, listing
> all U.S. foundations giving more
> than $200,000 per year and not
> restricted to local giving; updated
> monthly.

Foundation Grants to Individuals

> Lists programs of more than 1,000
> foundations, includes application
> information.

Foundation Grants Index

> Cumulated record of grants, including grants of $5000 or more, listed by state, subject recipient; check on projects similar to yours that have received grant aid.

Foundation Center National Data Book
1974-6, 2 vols.

> Brief information about 21,000 non-profit organizations classified as private foundations by IRS: lists information by name, amount of grants awarded annually, city, state and zip code location.

> Other sources of information about grants include:

About Foundations: How to Find the Facts You Need to Get a Grant
Judith B. Margolin
1975, 39 pp., also available through the Foundation Center

> Step-by-step suggestions on how to research grant sources.

Approaching Business for Support of the Arts
Business Committee for the Arts
1700 Broadway
New York 10029

> Includes information on more than 1,000 foundations and 300 corporations active in the arts, humanities and education.

The Art of Winning Foundation Grants
Howard Hillman and Karen Abarbanel
1975, 188 pp., $6.95
Vanguard Press
242 Madison Ave.
New York 10017

> Describes methods for getting grants
> from foundations; also presents sample
> proposal illustrating the principles
> of proposal writing.

Catalog of Federal Domestic Assistance
Superintendent of Documents
U.S. Government Printing Office
Washington DC 20402

> Detailed information on federal pro-
> grams of assistance or benefits to
> the public; includes more than 900
> programs, with information on grants,
> eligibility, applications, local
> contacts. Ask about other government
> documents in related areas.

Developing Skills in Proposal Writing
Mary Hall
Continuing Education Publications
1633 S.W. Park (PO Box 1491)
Portland OR 97207

Encyclopedia of Associations

> Source for information on grantmaking
> organizations that are not nonprofit;
> includes the organizations' objectives,
> publications, locations, officers.

340

*Grants: How to Find out About Them and
What to do Next*
Virginia P. White
1975, 354 pp.,
Plenum Press
227 W. 17 St.
New York 10011

> Discusses sources of information on
> government, foundation and corporate
> grants, with attention to writing
> proposals.

The Grantsmanship Center News
The Grantsmanship Center
1015 W. Olympic Blvd.
Los Angeles CA 90015

> Published 10 times per year at a
> subscription rate of $15, the paper
> offers articles on all aspects of
> obtaining grants.

*Grass Roots Fundraising Book: How to Raise
Money in Your Community*
1977
Swallow Press
811 W. Jr. Terrace
Chicago IL

Literature Program
National Endowment for the Arts
Washington DC 20506

> Gives grants to writers, literary
> magazines and presses; write for
> current information and application
> forms.

*Resource Directory for the Funding and
Managing of Non-Profit Organizations*
compiled by Ingrid Lemaire
Edna McConnell Clark Foundation
250 Park Ave., Rm. 900
New York

> Guide for nonprofit organizations,
> including information about funding
> sources, fundraising in general,
> research services, and organizations
> which provide management and technical
> services.

Reference Sources:

One of the most useful things you can do for yourself is become familiar with the reference section of your local library; just browsing on the shelves can acquaint you with an astonishing variety of fact-filled books that can assist you in various ways. Some of these include: *Facts on File: Weekly World News Digest with Cumulative Index, Reader's Guide to Periodical Literature, Statistical Abstract of the United States; Subject Directory of Special Libraries and Information Centers, Subject Guide to Books in Print.* In addition, check the library's list of U.s. Government Publications, or get yourself put on the regular mailing list by writing Supt. of Documents, U.S. Government Printing Office, Washington DC 20402; the government produces a staggering amount of inexpensive publications on every conceivable subject. You might also find the *Washington Information Directory*, or order it through interlibrary loan; it lists agencies, congressional committes and private associations based in Washington by subject.

Other reference sources to check include the following:

Illustration Index
Lucile E. Vance and Esther M. Tracey
(New York: Scarecrow Press, 1966)

Illustrations in magazines are listed, including photos and charts; you might use this to trace illustrations to borrow or rent.

Guide to Popular U.S. Government Publications
John L. Andriot
Documents Index
Box 453
Arlington 10, VA

Reference Books in Paperback: An Annotated Guide
Bolidan S. Wynar, ed.

Guide to Reference Books
American Library Association
Chicago, 1976

Best Reference Sources
Louis Shores

Reference Books: A Brief Guide
Mary N. Barton and Marion V. Bell
(Enoch Pratt Free Library, Publications Office, 400 Cathedral St., Baltimore MD 21201)

An introduction to selected reference books, divided into general and specific subjects, annotated.

The Concise Guide to Library Research
Grant W. Morse
(New York: Washington Square Press)

Writing, Revising:

Creative Writing in the Classroom
Robert Day, ed., Gail Cohen Weaver, assoc. ed.
National Council of Teachers of English
1111 Kenyon Rd
Urbana IL 61801

An annotated bibliography of selected
resources for grades K-12, covering
theory, practice and results of creative writing in the classroom; the
most applicable section for potential
publishers of student work is that con-
cerning anthologies of student work,
magazines that publish such work,
writing contests and the like; among
sources of special interest are:

"Encouraging Young Authors", Jack W.
Humphrey and Sandra R. Redden,
Reading Teacher 25 (April 1972):643-
51.

More than 3,000 children in Evans-
ville, IN wrote books or stories
which were bound, catalogued, and
placed in school libraries; con-
centrates primarily on methods used
to help children learn to write.

"Creative Writing in the Reading
Class", Anne B. Edelmen, *English
Journal* 65 (January 1975): 60-61.

Slow readers in 7th and 8th grades
wrote and bound their own books.

"For Our Book Fair, Pupils Were Authors", Reva Blotnick Rosen, *Instructor* 78 (April 1969): 70-71.

Children in all classes of an elementary school wrote, illustrated, bound and "published" books, which were displayed in a school book fair; includes tips on binding.

Guide to Rapid Revision
Daniel D. Pearlman and Paula R. Pearlman
(New York: Odyssey Press) 68 pp.

Handiest guide I've found for self-revision, written with clarity and simplicity so it's useful even in high schools; covers most common errors and how to correct them, without going into the more technical matters required by writers of dissertations and of no earthly use to the rest of us.

Appendix 10: Costs

Costs of *The Book Book:*

Supplies (approximate)
    paper, carbon ribbons
    correction tapes, scotch
    tape, paper
	$70

Press-type:	$22.27
Books:	$54.95

Postage:
    review copies of draft,
    interlibrary loan,
    inquiries
	$48

PMT's:	$86.85
Printing:	$3084
1200 paper $2064 300 cloth $1020	
Shipping costs (estimated)	$250
Total:	$3616.07

MEMBER

COSMEP

COMMITTEE OF SMALL MAGAZINE
EDITORS AND PUBLISHERS
BOX 703 SAN FRANCISCO, CA. 94101

The Last Word:

The instant one declares a book of this nature
finished, one is bound to turn up new information that really should be included. Some of
these additions can be made during pasteup,
but some can't, for reasons either of time or
space.

An addition I could not make was a definition
of the word "remainder". Major book publishers
take most books off their availability lists
within a few weeks after publication. Copies
remaining unsold are remaindered, bought very
cheaply by companies who specialize in selling
such books at cut rates, often by mail order.
Thus, though an author's book has been published
by a large company, it may be "out of print"
quickly. Copies still unsold by remaindering
are often shredded and made into paper for more
publishing. Reputable small publishers avoid
remaindering, and many guarantee that an author's
book will be available as long as printed copies
exist. This is an additional advantage to small
press publishing.

I'm already collecting material for a re-
vised edition; send corrections or additions to Lame Johnny Press

While I was pasting up final corrections for
this book, a propane heater beside my light
table exploded. Since the book's final copy
was camera-ready, loss of the pasteup in the
resulting fire would have been loss of two
years' work. I ran from the house with the
book BEFORE calling the fire department.
That's what happens to small press publishers.
Damage was most from smoke and fire extin-
guishers.

348